STORIES
FROM
AFIELD

Adventures with Wild
Things in Wild Places

BRUCE L. SMITH

University of Nebraska Press | Lincoln & London

Acknowledgments for the use of previously
published material appear on page 193, which
constitutes an extension of the copyright page.

Library of Congress Cataloging-in-Publication Data
Names: Smith, Bruce L., 1948– , author.
Title: Stories from afield: adventures with wild
things in wild places / Bruce L. Smith.
Description: Lincoln: University of Nebraska Press,
2016. | Series: Outdoor lives series.
Identifiers: LCCN 2016010714 (print)
LCCN 2016029455 (ebook)
ISBN 9780803288164 (pbk.: alk. paper)
ISBN 9780803295339 (epub)
ISBN 9780803295346 (mobi)
ISBN 9780803295353 (pdf)
Subjects: LCSH: Wildlife conservation—United
States—Fieldwork—Anecdotes. | Outdoor life—
United States—Anecdotes. | Smith, Bruce L., 1948–
Classification: LCC QL84.2 .s65 2016 (print) |
LCC QL84.2 (ebook) | DDC 333.95/40973—dc23
LC record available at
https://lccn.loc.gov/2016010714

Designed and set in Scala by L. Auten.

For Diana and my sisters, Norma and Sandy

Contents

Introduction   ix

 1. Snowbound   1

 2. Big Turtle   23

 3. The Way West   33

 4. The Deer Hunt   49

 5. The Elk Hunt   59

 6. Woodpeckers to Goats   73

 7. The Bear and the Tree   85

 8. Gravity   97

 9. Lightning   107

10. Collecting   115

11. Old Garbage Gut   129

12. In the Timber   137

13. Baby Elk   147

14. The Circle   161

15. Empty Forests   173

16. Four Decades Later   183

    Afterword   191

    Acknowledgments   193

Introduction

Some people just know at an early age what they want to do for the rest of their lives. It helps if you have a role model, maybe an influential teacher or relative, or are presented plenty of opportunities to explore life's possibilities. In my case, I think my lightning rod was my parents' decision to move to the country the summer I turned seven. It was that place that lit the fire. A wondrous mix of woodland, lake, and marsh where I had room to roam and the freedom to explore all that my new environment offered. An additional ingredient that can't be overstated is curiosity. That may be the one intangible that must come from within. It's also what has fueled my fascination with nature to the present.

So I consider myself one of the fortunate. I leveraged my childhood passion into a career as a wildlife biologist—an ongoing adventure living and working with nearly all the large mammal species of the western United States and in some of its grandest wildlands. From a life intertwined with wild things and wild places, I've drawn the following collection of stories. They begin with a childhood encounter with a monster snapping turtle and move on to finding my way from Michigan to the Rocky Mountain West and include an assortment of experiences I recount as a hunter, naturalist, and scientist pursuing birds and bears and elk and mountain goats.

I share these stories in hopes that you will experience some of the same joy, wonder, and drama I felt at those times. Along the way, you may discover a deeper connection and greater purpose in conserving the rich wild heritage we all share. And if the humor in humankind's frailty and unease amid wild nature amuses you, as it does me, so much the better.

STORIES FROM AFIELD

ONE

SNOWBOUND

Statistics are no substitute for judgment.

—Henry Clay

Long, cobalt silhouettes of junipers slipped beneath, as we chased our shadow across the dissected sagelands. An immature golden eagle sporting white-banded tail feathers, the decorative plumes prized by Plains Indians, streaked past the helicopter's left door. Dense, still air made for ideal flying conditions. It was a great day to be alive, soaring with the eagle.

Our pilot, John, guided the Hiller 12E around the east flank of Black Mountain. The peak's 10,087-foot, fir-cloaked hulk dominated the skyline. Behind Black Mountain lay Crow Creek basin, a pretty, willow-lined stream nestled between 11,000- to 12,000-foot-high Black Ridge on the west and Trail Ridge on the east. These joined to the north, forming an elongated horseshoe that fed Crow Creek's waters 2,000 to 3,000 feet below.

Our mission on this subzero morning in January 1980 was to survey elk, mule deer, and bighorn sheep in the Owl Creek Mountains of Wind River Indian Reservation in Wyoming. Along to help me was Rawley Friday. Rawley was Arapaho and a tribal game warden at the Wind River. About my height but stockier, he could handle himself. I liked flying with Rawley. He was devoted to the reservation's wildlife and a jovial companion on surveys; and he owned an iron stomach, something others I'd flown with didn't possess.

The prototype of the rotary-wing aircraft carrying us was built in 1944 by helicopter pioneer Stanley Hiller at the age of eighteen. Hiller Helicopters' first production aircraft, the Hiller UH12, first flew in 1948, the year I was born. By 1965 more than 2,300 were built for commercial and military use. The next rerun of *M.A.S.H.* you watch, look closely at the choppers used for medevac or to transport Hawkeye from the 4077 in the series finale. They are UH12s, first purchased by the military in 1950 as H-23 Ravens.

Like all reciprocating-engine craft, increasing altitude hampers performance. Our Hiller was equipped with a Soloy turbine conversion to ameliorate that limitation. The one drawback was the turbine's increased thirst for fuel, giving us only two to two and a half hours aloft per fill-up. We carefully planned the day's work with that in mind.

It was now midmorning. Nearly two hours had elapsed since Rawley and I met at the Thermopolis airport where our survey began. We'd already recorded 129 mule deer and almost 200 elk across the eastern three-fourths of the sixty-mile-long Owl Creek Range—improved numbers for that area compared to previous winters' counts. The high country loomed ahead.

In search of bighorn sheep along Trail and Black Ridges, we'd be operating at our highest altitudes on this final leg of the morning's flight. Unlike sheep in the reservation's Wind River Range to the southwest, which migrate to lower-elevation cliffs in winter, bighorns here wintered along wind-scoured ridgetops and escarpments. We carried another forty gallons of fuel in five-gallon jerricans in the Hiller's twin cargo baskets—one mounted on the skid beside each door. The additional weight would reduce performance at high altitudes, acting like ballast on a submarine, but avert a gas-guzzling ferry to refuel in Thermopolis. This dance of performance versus mission time vexes all remote mountain flights. But as one pilot told me, noting that far too many aviation accidents are caused by running out of fuel, "The only time there's too much fuel on a helicopter is when it's on fire."

The fuel gauge registered one-quarter full, as John throttled the Hiller toward Trail Ridge. We'd land on the ridgetop high above, refuel with the jerricans, and begin our hunt for bighorns.

As we approached Trail Ridge, John unexpectedly settled the Hiller in a foot of snow on the Crow Creek Road. His voice was tinged with concern as he said, "I want to check on something." Noting our probing expressions, he added, "I smelled something."

Weird sounds, vibrations, and smells can be telltale signs of trouble to a helicopter pilot, like the tingling sensation I'd felt in the Wind Rivers before lightning struck far too close. I'd not flown with John before, but this attention to detail eased my usual concern about new pilots. Other than being an oversized load for a chopper to lift at six foot three, John seemed competent at the controls. Without shutting the engine down, he climbed out through the flimsy, acrylic door and examined the Hiller's mechanics. In minutes, he was buckling into his shoulder harness, informing his onlooking passengers, "False alarm. Everything's okay." Rawley and I shared relieved looks. "Good," I said as the engine whined and snow whipped like meringue around the ship. "The closest service station's two days' hike from here."

As the Hiller whooshed forward, Rawley and I resumed scanning for big critters or their recent passage from telltale tracks. It was midwinter. A storm had dumped fresh snow—conditions that maximized visibility of game and covered old animal tracks. Any new ones would likely lead us to whatever animals made them.

The Hiller strained and shuddered upward into a world above ten thousand feet that was snowbound, except for stunted treetops, cliffs, and shreds of windblown ridge. This was the windiest area of the reservation. Funneling eastward off the Continental Divide through the Wind River valley, winds howled unobstructed before encountering Black Ridge. On windward slopes and ridgetops, velocities could be brutal. On the leeward flanks, turbulence was particularly dangerous, sometimes insane. In sum, advancing weather fronts made surveying game impossible. Today, high pressure had settled over Wyoming, bringing favorable conditions. Yet John was busy at the foot pedals adjusting for the swirling gusts that yanked the tail boom left then right.

We intended to refuel along the crest of Trail Ridge near Monument Peak, at whatever spot offered a level landing site. The upsurge in wind now threatened that design. A misstep along the ridge's narrow spine could make for an untidy landing. A rogue downdraft or wind shear could prove disastrous. John nudged the Hiller up the west side of Trail Ridge. The ship sailed skyward on updrafts and then yawed sideways as the air settled beneath the rotary wing and buffeted the fuselage. Gaining the ridgetop, the Hiller suddenly banked west across Crow Creek basin. "Thwack, thwack, thwack!" Through the noise-dampening padding of my flight helmet, the main rotor pounded like a jackhammer.

Sensing our intense stares, John announced, "We better look for a landing site somewhere below the ridgetop. Somewhere the winds are more manageable than up here."

The other option, descending more than two thousand feet to Crow Creek to refuel, would cost us precious fuel to regain our eleven-thousand-foot altitude. Neither John nor I wanted to do that. We circled back and scanned the bleak landscape below the ridge crest.

"Maybe there!" John jutted his chin forward.

Rawley and I peered in that direction and back at John's eyes for confirmation. "That spot?" Rawley questioned.

Just above the altitudinal limits of the subalpine fir belt, our eyes converged on the only level perch—more like a possibility of a landing spot. A spur off Trail Ridge descended some two hundred feet to a modest platform and then plunged to Crow Creek far below. The flat was snowbound, like everything else, but offered a landing perch large and stable enough for the petite helicopter to roost . . . or so we reassured ourselves. Fresh avalanches shredded Trail Ridge's winter mantle to our left and right. Tons of snow had plunged hundreds of feet in some slides. A spasm of unease clutched my chest.

John circled twice more to gauge the winds. "You okay with this?" he purposefully asked, not taking his eyes off the mountain and the fast-approaching treetops.

The fuel gauge had dipped below one-quarter. From just one hundred feet above, the little lz looked safe enough to me.

"Yeah," I replied and glanced at Rawley for signs of reluctance. "Let's do it."

A brief lull in the wind aided our approach. Into the snow the Hiller settled nearly fuselage-deep. The cargo baskets buoyed it from sinking further. As the turbine engine wound down, the three of us unbuckled our harnesses and stepped onto the cargo baskets' framework and then thigh-deep into powder. Bucking the snow, Rawley and I removed the bungees and ferried the jerricans to John, who emptied the contents of each through its flexible pour spout into the fuel tank. Another two hours of flight time awaited—enough to thoroughly survey the twenty miles of lofty horseshoe surrounding Crow Creek and Mountain Meadows below and then return to Thermopolis with a helping tailwind.

Back in the Hiller, we rebuckled harnesses, squeezed heads into helmets, and connected dangling avionics plugs. John summoned on the intercom, "Ready?"

Rawley and I each replied, "Ready."

"Clear!" John announced and fired the turbine, which after several tries rumbled to life. Sluggishly at first and then with increasing authority, the Hiller rose from our perch, as great eddies of snow engulfed us.

When a helicopter lifts off, it begins so in HIGE—that's chopperese for "hover in ground effect." This signifies a condition of optimal performance encountered when operating near the ground. A helicopter requires less power to achieve the same amount of lift near the ground, because the ground interrupts the airflow beneath the helicopter, reducing downward velocity of the airflow, translating to more vertical lift. Essentially, a compacted cushion of air between the rotary wing and the ground supports and lifts the chopper. Once a height exceeding one rotor diameter is reached, the helicopter transitions to HOGE, or "hover out of ground effect." A pilot will then increase the angle of attack, or the rotor blades' forward tilt, to develop forward-moving speed. Continuous, coordinated adjustments to the throttle, foot pedals, cyclical, and collective controls keep the contraption from gyrating aimlessly.

I mention this not to impress you with my elementary grasp of aviation physics but to illustrate a point. Flying a helicopter is a complex affair, demanding a pilot's constant attention. Airplanes are designed to land on runways or, in the case of float planes, on water. Doing otherwise isn't impossible. Airplanes can land on roads, fields, and less suitable locations in a pinch. Alaskan bush pilots land most anywhere they can. Larry Hastings once landed me on a faint two-track road near Crowheart Butte in his Cessna 182. We both had to pee so badly, after too much coffee and nearly four hours of counting pronghorn antelope, that bladder damage seemed imminent.

Helicopters are designed to land at unimproved landing sites. Think of some butt-puckering situation—a pocket of grass pressed between towering firs, an old burn strewn with snags and downed trees, or a sage-covered hillside demanding a one-skid touch-and-go in a gale—and some pilot has landed there. Such landings I'd survived in Viet Nam I considered heroic. In natural resource work (fire-fighting and rescue work in particular), they happen as regularly. It's just that in civilian employment, rarely are folks shooting at you.

Ours was not the classic takeoff I described three paragraphs earlier. John executed a variation, God bless him. Maybe because we were perched on this little launch pad so near an abruptly rising slope; maybe because the swirling snow hampered visibility; maybe because he wanted to clear all danger before turning the helicopter into the wind; or maybe because of some technical aspect that I probably couldn't explain, if I knew it. I don't know the reason—never thought to ask him.

Instead, John took the Hiller skyward, without dropping the nose to gather forward speed. We went straight up. Up, briefly . . . until we fell from the sky. Not like a rock, rather like the autorotation that another pilot had demonstrated on a flight a year earlier. In fact, that's what the Hiller did. It autorotated right back to our launch pad, with a jolt and a billow of snow.

It happened so quickly that I didn't have time to get terrified. Although every time I've thought about it since, my heart zips a bit. Ten yards to one side or the other and we'd have alighted beyond that flat spot on the spur ridge and then begun sliding and tumbling creek bound. The dense stand of firs just below would have halted our descent, but the damage caused by the rotor blades battering the mountainside would be done by then. Picture locking an industrial Mixmaster on high speed, releasing the handle, and then watching it dance from a countertop onto the floor . . . only way more dramatic. Helicopter rotor blades are huge. Each measures almost eighteen feet in length on the Hiller. And at full-throttle revolution that's needed to lift the ship and passengers from the ground, they wield tremendous force.

We might have survived, if the cabin remained intact. I don't know the fracture resistance of the acrylic canopy or the tensile strength of the supporting metal alloy structure. It would surely have been tested that day. Fire is the other life-threatening danger, particularly for unconscious or disabled passengers unable to escape from safety harnesses.

None of these "could haves" happened. We plopped right back where we had been moments before. Rawley and I looked wide-eyed at each other and then at John.

"What happened?" I started.

"Lost the fuel pump," John said. "Just conked out!"

"The fuel pump!" Rawley exclaimed, paused, and then inquired further. "Can ya' fix it?"

"I don't know. Probably not here." John replied.

I looked at my watch. It was 11:30—plenty of time to check out the fuel pump, fix it, and resume our work. It must be repairable, I resolved. We were snowbound at ten thousand feet and miles from anywhere.

Everyone unbuckled and got out as the rotor blades spun down. "Whoop, whooop, whooooop." Their tips assumed a sad, lifeless droop. John rummaged in the tail boom's stowage compartment and came out with a small toolbox. He climbed up to the engine and fiddled with something for a few minutes while Rawley and I watched and asked a couple of pointless questions. When John stepped down into the cargo basket, he looked grimly past us.

"Let's get back inside," he ordered.

When John triggered the ignition, the engine sputtered but failed to fire. Again he tried, to no avail, and then blurted, "No way. Can't be fixed here. Most likely, it will need replacing."

I felt the air go out of my lungs. My first concern was that we wouldn't complete today's survey. The second was that we probably wouldn't be finishing up tomorrow either. And third, I wondered how long before we would be rescued. That's the thought that stuck.

Before we climbed back into the cabin, I got my daypack out of the stowage compartment. I had water, a sandwich, gorp, and a chocolate bar in there, along with gaiters and a parka strapped to the outside. Flying in the heated helicopter, it was too warm to wear the down parka. It sure was welcome now.

Inside, Rawley and I removed our flight helmets. I replaced mine with a stocking hat. Rawley donned a blue wool cap with earflaps. John fingered the radio switch, adjusted his helmet's mike, and tried to raise the Riverton or Lander airports. "Lander Unicom, this is helicopter . . ."

He repeated the transmissions a dozen times. No response. He glanced at us, probably wondering what we were wondering. Then he retuned the radio to another frequency, the Mayday channel. The contrail of a jetliner was passing overhead. His determined efforts to raise a reply were again fruitless.

He wrenched the helmet from his head and offered a couple of choice expressions . . . the insightful kind appropriate for our now-apparent predicament. He turned to us and said, "We have no radio contact. The avionics must have been damaged when we landed."

The radio antenna was buried in the snow compacted beneath the fuselage. Even if we dug it out, John replied to my inquiry, it would make no difference. I recall disliking his defeated tone. Rawley and I were willing to dig, excavate, burrow—whatever was needed. But John's further explanation of the problem convinced us that digging was just a good way to get soaked and then good and cold—a surefire formula for hypothermia.

I recall the sun beaming through the clear canopy. It felt warm on my face at its midday zenith. But in five hours, it would sink behind the Wind Rivers; and the air temperature along with it. The morning forecast on the Lander AM radio station called for twenty degrees below zero tonight. That was at 5,400 feet elevation, not here at 10,000. The helicopter's round thermometer showed just twelve degrees on the plus side now. Without an insulating cloud layer, tonight's temperature would be bitter.

John tried the radio again as I mulled our options. I knew that convention dictated remaining with the aircraft in the event of an accident. Search craft would look for the downed Hiller, guided by the onboard ELT, or emergency locator transmitter. Every airplane and helicopter is equipped with one. A crash landing's impact activates the ELT, which emits a radio pulse signal on the 121.5-megahertz frequency. ELTs can be manually activated also. John did so, recognizing that our moderate impact may not have done the job. Aircraft monitoring the ELT frequency, and flying near enough to receive it, would be alerted to our emergency. Great! We would be rescued—as soon as somebody knew we needed rescuing.

These were the days before the federal Office of Aviation Services required flight following of government-chartered craft—fifteen-minute-interval communications between small aircraft and radio base stations. Before those requirements were implemented in the 1990s, dozens of pilots and passengers in downed airplanes and helicopters may have been saved had their accidents not belatedly been detected. Over my thirty-year career, seven of my colleagues would lose their lives while conducting wildlife surveys or radiotelemetry missions. A small plane carrying one disappeared over the Arctic Ocean during a polar bear census. Another went down in some Arizona mountains while surveying desert bighorn sheep. Two fixed-wing pilots, with whom I would log many hours tracking radioed elk, died on ill-fated missions just days after I'd flown with each. Still others died in helicopter crashes. And another wildlife student I accompanied on my first wildlife flight back in graduate school—the flight that introduced me to the fundamentals of aerial radiotelemetry—died a few weeks later. The Super Cub in which he was radio-tracking elk augured into a dense stand of Montana lodgepole pine. It wasn't found for two weeks. All of these, and many more flights that took the lives of biologists and wardens and pilots I never knew, testified to the danger of this aspect of wildlife work.

In most incidents of downed aircraft, time is of the essence. The only exception, of course, is when there are no survivors. Injured passengers may suffer shock, blood loss, life-threatening trauma, and the risk of death due to exposure. The clock starts ticking immediately. The first twenty-four hours are critical. The sooner that help arrives and the injured can receive medical treatment, the greater their chances of surviving. Rapid detection of a crash is critical.

We were *so* fortunate. The three of us suffered no injuries. But I knew that a night spent at tonight's temperatures—likely thirty below zero—spelled hypothermia. I also knew the following. Rawley had mentioned to the aviation tech who fueled the Hiller in Thermopolis that we were doing a wildlife survey toward East Fork of the Wind River. But he probably wouldn't report our failure to return for fuel. It wasn't his responsibility. My office wouldn't become alarmed until after nightfall, because I planned other fieldwork after our flight. John had filed a general flight plan, "a five-hour wildlife survey in the Owl Creek Mountains," with his employer, Hawkins and Powers Aviation, before leaving Greybull, Wyoming, an hour-plus distance from here by airplane. When would H&P consider that John was overdue in Greybull? Finally, our exact location in this sixty-mile-long mountain range would take time to pinpoint, should our ELT fail. I learned later that ELT failure rate was disconcertingly high.

But most disturbing, I learned that the standard winter emergency equipment—food, water, sleeping bags, and snowshoes—were missing from the Hiller's stowage compartment. Besides the toolbox John retrieved, the compartment contained only a flare gun, an oil-soaked blanket, and nothing else. *Why?* A serious oversight on someone's part. With three sleeping bags to crawl inside or even a couple to drape around us, night would have been bearable, at worst survivable. Considering these grim circumstances, I was contemplating another plan.

After a half hour of unanswered radio transmissions and sharing my gorp and water with the others, I was ready for action. Even in pac boots, I could already feel my toes chilling with inactivity in the unheated cockpit. Countless days in too-tight hockey skates on Michigan lakes and outdoor rinks had taken a toll on my circulation. With the sun arcing westward and twenty more hours until tomorrow's sunrise, time was wasting.

Rawley and I shared the same thoughts. Neither of us was keen on death by freezing. "I think we oughta hike outta here," I said.

Rawley's nod brought a strident protest from John, "We should all stay together, all stay with the helicopter. That's where they'll look for us."

I agreed with the first part. Sticking together was imperative, whether we stayed or left. I just believed we should all hike out, helping each other as needed. Rawley and I knew from the maps I carried that the nearest help was the Duncan place, a ranch on East Fork of the Wind River that flowed along the reservation's west boundary. We also knew that it was far below us and twelve miles west. A reasonable task in summer, I thought, but certainly an ordeal in untracked snow and without snowshoes. Furthermore, part of the slog would happen after dark, even if we set out right away.

On the plus side, after dropping two thousand feet down Trail Ridge to Crow Creek, there was a two-track to follow the entire way to East Fork. Sure, it would be snowbound, but nonetheless an obvious course. Rawley had traveled those tracks since childhood. I had driven them a couple of times in summer. We also knew that just two miles south of where we'd intercept the two-track paralleling Crow Creek, a cowboy cabin was nestled beside the creek. Make it there, start a fire in the potbellied stove, and we'd be comfy.

The debate wore on. John insisted that a search craft would soon be wheeling overhead. My mind was racing with more pessimistic scenarios. I argued that if it were a fixed-wing rather than a helicopter, we'd have to wait an hour more for a helicopter. Then there was no assurance a helicopter could land up here after dark. And what if a search effort wasn't dispatched today or didn't find us, for any number of reasons? Even without the service of snowshoes, I knew I was fit enough to trek out.

John shivered. His leather aviator jacket was lighter than our parkas. I took that as a sign that this forty-something former LAPD pilot dreaded the prospect of enduring a night at thirty below. He was weakening to option B.

Rawley and I shared the logistics of the undertaking. "We'll follow this spur ridge down to Crow Creek," I penciled the least grueling route down Trail Ridge on the map.

"Jim Hill's cabin is about here," Rawley pointed. "The mice won't mind some company."

"The Duncan place is over here. It's the first place where we'll find help," I added as John's eyes widened at its distance from the cabin.

"I don't know," John hesitated, clearly conflicted. "You sure there's a cabin there?" he questioned Rawley. "I don't see it on the map, like the Duncan place."

"Yeah, right about here," Rawley pointed. Then eyeballing him, he added, "They don't put every little shack on these maps."

"John, this is doable," I assured him.

Minutes later, we all plunged into the thigh-deep snow, secured the helicopter rotor with the tie strap, and set out. Despite the effort of slogging through bottomless powder, gravity would be our ally. It was all downhill to Crow Creek.

♣

I broke trail. Rawley and John followed in the furrow I plowed through the snow. I couldn't decide if it was harder to raise each foot nearly out of the snow before plunging it forward again or just to push the snow forward with my legs as I gained another two feet per stride. So I alternated between the two routines. No score for style points here.

Within minutes, we were all breathing hard. We had covered barely two hundred yards—*maybe* twenty minutes of toiling—when Rawley shouted, "Hold up!"

He enjoyed fry bread and other Arapaho fare not generally considered health food. Although well proportioned, he was an outdoorsman and younger than John and me. I expected him to keep pace or maybe trade off the lead, so I was surprised when he called for me to stop. I turned to see him a few yards back supporting John, who was bent and clutching his leg.

"You doing okay?" I called.

"Damn cramp in my leg," John grimaced.

I trudged back and located the outline of a downed tree mounded with snow. I brushed it off, and Rawley helped John to it. Sitting hunched on the log, John began rubbing his aching left hamstring. After a few minutes, he said he felt better, and we continued on.

Another ten minutes and John cried out. He'd cramped again. Rawley and I helped him to another log that we cleared. This time, John was really hurting. Both hamstrings were agonizingly cramping, and he was gasping for air. He began massaging one leg, and I offered to help with the other. I unzipped my parka and retrieved the quart water bottle from an inside cargo pocket. I'd filled the half-empty bottle with snow before we left the helicopter. Eating snow can ward off dehydration, but it can also reduce core temperature and hasten hypothermia. I hoped to thwart those effects by hastening the snowmelt with my body heat. Guessing that John was dehydrated, I encouraged him to drink freely of the bottle's slushy contents.

The muscles in John's legs were bound in knots. Kneading gradually relaxed the tightness in his hamstrings. John thanked us profusely for our forbearance, apologized for holding us up, and said he was ready to continue. This scenario repeated itself periodically. When he was moving, we made decent progress. He just wasn't moving consistently, repeatedly hesitating to catch his breath and stroke his thighs. Standing six foot three, John sported legs rivaling a *Star Wars* Imperial Walker. With legs that long, he should have handled snow like a bull moose. Instead, they were a bane, afflicted with excruciating cramps. He was obviously not rehydrating, or else his physical conditioning just sucked. Whichever, our progress was agonizingly slow.

Somewhere down the mountain, Rawley's eyes and mine locked. Neither of us spoke, yet we read each other's thoughts. *If I had any idea that he'd be this slow* . . . Sooner than expected, nightfall would engulf us. Nonetheless, there was no hint of doubt in either of our faces. We were both committed to going on, especially now that the helicopter was hundreds of feet above us. Returning to the Hiller was *not* an option.

So on we went, ever downward, as the sun receded southwest toward the dazzling summits of the Wind Rivers. Eventually the dimly lit pine and fir gave way to russet and golden willow thickets demarcating the course of Crow Creek. "Doin' okay, John?" Rawley called as he and I waited at the forest margin. Miles from the nearest combusting engine or humming powerline, only John's labored breathing and the swoosh of feet through snow breached the stillness. We *had* to reassess our situation.

"We've got two choices," I rationalized. "We can either continue on together and hope to get Hopalong to the cowboy cabin before we're all spent . . ."

"Or," Rawley interrupted, "before he has a heart attack."

"Or we can split up," I whispered, as John's panting grew louder, "one of us stay with John, the other hoof it to the Duncan place." The ranch's snow machines would get assistance into Crow Creek in no time. If the worst happened, we could bundle John in a sled and tow him behind one of the machines. Nine miles, the distance I estimated from the maps, was nothing by Arctic Cat.

Rawley and I looked at each other a long moment, gazed toward the rosy summits of the Winds, and back toward John's raspy approach. Neither of us wanted to make the call.

Finally, Rawley spoke. "I'll stay with John. You go ahead."

"You sure?" I asked.

"Yeah. You're in better shape than me. You'll be faster," he grinned.

I sipped the remaining liquid and then thrust the plastic bottle and squashed sandwich I'd retrieved from my daypack toward him. "You'll need this more than me. You can fill the bottle in Crow Creek." Rawley refused but with some prodding acquiesced. He took the bottle, casting a glance at John's humped figure emerging cheerlessly from the forest. "You keep the sandwich," he resolutely replied, refusing to take it.

We explained our intentions to John, calmly detailing our logic. He objected only mildly, embarrassed by his part in our predicament. One last encouragement to both, and I slipped into the willows.

Along Crow Creek, the snow was still fluffy and barely knee-deep. I wove through the tangled stems lining the creek and stopped for a long pull where water bubbled through a gap between ice-covered rocks. It was mouth-numbing, but I drank as much as I could until my scalp began to ache. I found the road along the west side, where a porcupine had left the telltale drag of its tail. I veered south. The remaining eleven miles from here to East Fork were gently downhill. I'd make good time, if my energy held out.

I reflexively swung one pac boot and then the other through the scattering snow. The adrenaline was pumping nicely. I forced myself to concentrate on what I needed to do. Still, I couldn't avoid stewing about how the others would fare, if splitting up was the right decision, and whether I would find someone home at the Duncan place. *How far was the next closest ranch?* Those thoughts conspired to distract me from the long trek ahead.

In less than an hour, I covered the two miles to the road junction where I turned west and left Crow Creek behind. I couldn't see the cabin but knew it lay just a short distance downstream. I considered going there myself, getting a fire burning in the stove, and heading back to help Rawley. I thought better of it. That's not what we decided, and for good reason. If John's cramping and exhaustion worsened, he'd be better served the sooner I got him help.

🌲

It was shortly after 5:00 p.m. The snow now matched the height of my ten-inch boots. I paused to take in the last light glowing crimson atop Trail Ridge behind me. Searching, I couldn't spot the Hiller, which was apparently concealed by fir trees or their inky shadows. I mouthed several scoops of snow, allowing my tongue to rewarm after each. Suddenly, I began to salivate, remembering the Milky Way bar tucked in my pack. The sandwich long since devoured, I had hoarded this final item for a later time when those 250 calories might prove vital. Now seemed as vital a time as any.

Just ahead I noticed a single set of elk tracks crossing the roadway. As the last of the chocolate and caramel dissolved in my mouth, I saw where the elk had pawed and cropped Indian ricegrass, identifiable from its airy seed stalks. Over there a fringed sage had been nibbled, leaving the animal's nose imprint pressed in the snow. The tracks meandered and vanished into the indigo snow at last light. Past the shadows and stillness, my thoughts reenacted the timeless pounding of hooves.

Following the somber silhouettes of sage and rabbitbrush down the snowmelt-scoured terraces to the Big Wind River, and continuing along the river's cottonwood gallery forest through badlands and prairies, I envisioned the ancient migrations of buffalo across the centuries. Gracing the breadth of the Great Plains, the great herds thundered and pulsed in nomadic rhythms in concert with winter storms and summer rains. Behind them on foot and then mounted on painted ponies, the hunters likewise shadowed the seasons and processions of *boha-guchu* (Shoshone for bison).

Over the intervening century, the migration trails had faded or were trampled to dust by their beef-bearing cousins. Now restoring these largest of native herbivores seemed as unlikely as the return of wooly mammoths. The stockman's disdain for competition and the bison's penchant to roam to the horizons—without regard for rivers or roads, fences or farms—had sealed their modern-day fate. Only in Yellowstone Park, Jackson Hole, and Utah's Henry Mountains were remnant U.S. herds given license to live unconfined. Unlike the Wind River's resident elk, deer, and pronghorn, the buffalo and the Native American economy it nourished had vanished forever.

Why did *I* mourn that world's eclipse? They were not my ancestors, neither the buffalo nor their pursuers. Being raised on the shores of Muskegon Lake (the Ottawa Indian term *Masquigon* means "marshy river") provided me no nurturing connection to Native people I'd never met. *Maybe*, I mused, *I was hardwired with compassion for all fellow creatures.* Not likely! I could be as insensitive as anyone else. Instead, I concluded that my feelings arose from common purpose. My work and time among the Shoshone and Arapaho people fostered this bond with their present situation and veneration for their past. Glancing toward Black Mountain's towering hulk, I felt deeply thankful for this opportunity I'd been granted.

Squinting at the cloven imprints left not long ago, I considered how comfortable the elk was in this environment. Her night vision, superb hearing, and sense of smell, I could only envy. Insulated by subcutaneous fat, a thick hide, dense underfur, and a weather-repellant outer coat of hollow guard hair, the elk was well suited to a life among the elements. I, on the other hand, felt like a vulnerable speck beneath the eternal night sky on this lonely frozen land.

With no concern for my welfare, I'd left Rawley and John in the gathering dusk. Now for the first time, thoughts skittered through my head that are material for fictional thrillers. Somewhere in the night, mountain lions roamed the canyons and forests, seeking prey my size and larger. *But you've traveled alone in lion country many times before*, I chided. My graduate studies of mountain goats found me mountaineering and camping days at a time miles from anyone among the peaks and snowfields atop the Selway-Bitterroot Wilderness Area. All that was different now was my itinerant imagination. Besides, things could be worse. The black and grizzly bears that frequented this region were sequestered in their winter dens, fast asleep.

While I was moving, the swoosh of each step drowned the silence—that place where creatures of the night abide. Still as a fence post now, I remained a captive of the ethereal peacefulness a moment longer. I listened to the night and thought I could as well be among the hovering stars.

I stirred with a shiver. It was cold, very cold. Well below zero, I ventured. The wind had long since failed, for which I was grateful. Exposed as my route was, a bitter windchill would have mercilessly sapped me. Still, my breath caked my beard and mustache with icicles. *Time to get hustling*, the voice within implored. To some internal cadence, following one track of the road and then the other, I methodically plodded along.

It must have been seven o'clock when what sounded like the faint drone of an engine pierced the hush. Not the drum of a helicopter but the steady hum of a fixed-wing headed somewhere through the night. Reflexively staring in the sound's direction, I strained to determine if it might be drawing closer. Nothing marred the cloudless sky except a low-riding moon and a multitude of stars that coalesced in one brilliant swath as the Milky

Way. *Mmmm, Milky Way.* My stomach clutched at the thought. The hum faded away. I didn't belabor the possibilities.

I turned back toward the Big Dipper, my guidepost to guard against a haphazard choice at occasional two-track intersections. Pulling my flashlight from a cargo pocket, I rechecked my progress on the Crow Mountain quadrangle. I reserved the light for periodic inspections of the map—just in case I should need it later for unforeseen circumstances. Buoyed by the fact that barely two miles remained to my destination, I stuffed the map and flashlight back in the parka. Then I heard it again—the mounting drone of the engine.

As the resonance swelled, the sky burst into crimson light, and the trailing glow of a flare floated earthbound. The craft audibly responded, though I saw only a blinking green light several miles to the east. My face flushed with emotion.

"They made it." I mouthed. Rawley and John were okay.

I felt momentarily conflicted. I was far closer to the Duncan place but drawn backward to the cabin. *No. Stay with the plan.* The airplane merely established our location. A helicopter or a search party on snowmobiles was needed to reach the remote cabin. I pushed ahead with renewed spring in my legs.

🌲

Well after dark, Rawley and John reached the cabin. John was all in. Wheezing, pale, and wracked by leg spasms, he tumbled onto the bare coil-spring bed positioned along one wall of the ten-foot-by-ten-foot shack. There he sprawled, kneading his legs, while Rawley inspected the wood-burning stove. Finding no firewood inside, he went to the livestock corral and tore loose several of the thinnest fence rails. He broke them in pieces and started a fire. Now more than ever, he considered John a heart attack waiting to happen. If no rescuers arrived by daylight, he planned to stoke the fire and follow my tracks to the Duncan place.

From inside, Rawley heard the whisper of an engine. He bolted through the door. John joined him outside and produced the red flare gun from his jacket. Minutes after the night sky above the cabin exploded crimson, the Cessna buzzed the cabin and wagged its wings. John knew that in moments from the home base in Greybull a helicopter would be dispatched to rescue them.

An hour later, the "thwack, thwack, thwack" of changing rotor pitch echoed off Trail Ridge. A searchlight advanced and then panned about where I guessed the cowboy cabin rested. The light glided downward until extinguished by the low ridge I'd just descended.

It was after eight o'clock when the cadence of rotor blades returned. A searchlight traced my footsteps. Shortly, I climbed through a rear door of the Jet Ranger, reunited with the others. As we lifted skyward, an amber yard light glimmered a mile west at the Duncan place. I'd been hiking for nearly eight hours and felt like it.

We were back at Thermopolis in twenty minutes, as if nothing had happened out of the ordinary. Nothing, that is, except a stern reproach from both pilot and copilot that we should have remained with the Hiller. The ELT's signal had activated. The Cessna had searched for us there first and then spotted the flare at the cabin. While their efforts to find us were mightily welcome, none of us was in the mood for the ass chewing we received.

"What were you thinking?" Dan Hawkins scolded. "You of all people should know to stay with the helicopter, John!"

Well, personally I was thinking warmth, food, water—maybe survival—all of which I was on my way to securing, had a helicopter rescue not occurred that night. But no need to prolong the chitchat, I thought. All's well that ends well. Besides, I felt too exhausted to argue the point. *But before my next helicopter ride, I'll make sure there is survival gear on board. What about that, guys?*

TWO

BIG TURTLE

Behold the turtle. He makes progress
only when he sticks his neck out.

—James Bryant Conant

During the summer I turned seven, my parents gave me what became the greatest gift I could receive. They bought their first home on the north shore of Muskegon Lake in western Michigan. From a two-bedroom in-town rental sandwiched among other houses, they moved their young family of five to the countryside. How they afforded it on the salaries of a traveling candy salesman and a bookkeeper, I marvel at now.

In western Michigan, it's hard to be in the middle of nowhere. And we weren't. But by comparison, our new home seemed like it to me. The woodlot across the street was habitat for rabbits, fox, deer, and flying squirrels. Rimming the lake behind our house, a large cattail marsh brimmed with all manner of life.

Aside from the Great Lakes, Michigan is blessed with hundreds of smaller inland lakes. Muskegon Lake is one of the largest, stretching two miles across and five miles long. With a connecting channel to Lake Michigan, it serves as the largest port along the east shore of the Big Lake. Muskegon itself is a big enough lake to send most runabouts and ski boats scurrying for shore whenever a storm rolls in from Lake Michigan.

But what captivated me as a kid were the bays, shallows, and marshes along Muskegon Lake's margins. These were great breeding grounds for ducks, snipe, songbirds, muskrats, and mink and food-rich environments for fish and a variety of frogs, snakes, and turtles.

This was a place where "nature deficit disorder" was absent and a time (the 1950s) before the term "stranger danger" was coined. Beyond what bruises and scrapes we'd come home with next, my parents' only concerns were that my sisters and I were not late for dinner and after that were home by nightfall, unless, of course, we had a good excuse: the fishing was especially good or Johnny's boat motor ran out of gas or . . . My immersion in outdoor adventure, rather than video games and YouTube clips, was healthy for body and mind and cultivated a deep connection to the land and nature. I believe that freedom to explore was the spark that fired my fascination with wild things and the mysteries of how they lived. E. O. Wilson writes of this same zeal for discovering how nature works in his memoir, *Naturalist*, a compelling read about the roots of his conservation career. It doesn't require a grand landscape or wilderness to prime the pump. A nearby pond or anthill will often do.

Circumstances, surroundings, and mentoring all play their part, yet it takes something more to shape a conservation career or instill a life-long passion for wild nature. That something extra must come from within, an inborn curiosity coded in a child's DNA.

🌲

From that first summer at age seven, I became a self-taught student of my new neighborhood environment. The curriculum included catching and collecting wild critters. Mucking around in marshes; traipsing through woodlands; and assembling a small zoo of reptiles, amphibians, and assorted "creepy crawlies" opened nature's doors to me.

My mother, who had little use for the things I brought home, surrendered the second stall of our garage to crates of snakes and tubs of frogs, crayfish, and turtles. Though they were banned from the house, she accepted my charges, even reminding me of their feeding schedules. However, the summer day that I decided to "exercise" half a dozen snakes simultaneously, I learned her limits. Freed from their homemade wooden-and-screened confinement, the snakes scattered in every direction across our backyard. Like the wild things they were, they slithered back toward where they belonged.

In a panic, I yelled to my mother in the house. Probably thinking I had inflicted some dreadful injury on myself, she bolted to my rescue, only to find a two-foot hognose snake at her feet. No, I couldn't persuade her to help retrieve the fleeing fugitives. Still, she suppressed her revulsion and directed me to each one, until all but my prized ribbon snake were safely impounded again.

During those formative years that I spent exploring marshes—mapping muskrat houses and red-winged blackbird nests and fishing for bluegills, largemouth bass, and dogfish—I developed a special fondness for turtles. They were abundant and fairly easy to catch. They also did well in captivity on a diet of bugs, minnows, lettuce, and raw hamburger meat. I tended, fed, and admired these beasts, even selling a few at a herpetological roadside stand to tourists and a professor from the University of Michigan. "Big ones 25¢, little ones 35¢," my turtles-for-sale sign read (like puppies, little ones were in greater demand). I was naïve to any ethical concerns, and my parents didn't discourage my entrepreneurial penchant.

These prehistoric creatures, living holdovers of the Mesozoic Era, are true evolutionary novelties. Their construction—muscles and organs sandwiched between two oblong dinner plates—is an anatomical gamble that has changed little in 220 million years, more ancient in origin than lizards, snakes, and crocodiles. Some 250 species of these reptiles inhabit oceans, lakes, streams, forests, and even deserts around the globe. Such longevity and geographic distribution attest success in the contest of natural selection.

And those dinner plates, more accurately called the carapace and plastron—or the upper and lower shells, as most of us know them—come in a variety of sizes, shapes, textures, and colors, all of which help distinguish each species. From the highly decorative, eight-inch shells of painted turtles to the six-foot-long, 1.5-inch-thick armaments of leatherback sea turtles, they provide a host of variations on a common theme—an organic suit of armor that the reptile lives inside.

The tortoises are land-dwelling cousins of the turtles. Some carry size and shape to extreme, like those ancient inhabitants of the Galapagos Islands that fascinated Charles Darwin more than 180 years ago. Just as the beaks and niches of thirteen species of finches varied across the archipelago, the assorted, high-domed carapaces he observed and sketched of the tortoises on each Galapagos island were not lost on the young British naturalist.

As an asset to survival, the shell has proven successful over the millennia. Its protective function outweighs the drawback of lugging its weight wherever turtles swim and tortoises shamble. This makes all the more remarkable the carapaces of the widespread soft-shelled turtles, such as those we called "rubber-backs" in western Michigan.

♣

Muskegon Lake was home to several kinds of turtles. There were painted turtles, of course, North America's most ubiquitous species, and greenish-tan map turtles, which the neighborhood kids called "sun turtles" for their love of basking. There were also musk turtles; red-eared sliders; and those beguiling, tube-nosed rubber-backs, which could rival a washtub in size.

But among our lake's inhabitants, the snapping turtle intrigued me most. That name, the black color, a vicious set of slicing jaws, and a Darth Vader–like predatory disposition made a kid wade with caution into Muskegon Lake's murky shallows. The first indication of a snapper's presence was often when a fist-sized head poked through the veneer of frog spit (properly called duckweed) skimming the marsh's dark waters in the heat of summer. Encounters with something that scary just seem to stick in the memory bank.

It was my first year at the lake house. Along with thirty or so first and second graders, I attended the one-room schoolhouse down the road. There was no school bus. Getting to school each day meant walking or riding our bikes, over a half mile for some of us.

As if it happened yesterday, I recall an adventure not long before the school year ended. It remains lodged in my memory along with the January day when someone dared me to lick a steel support post of the playground's swing set.

Green Creek School was perched beside a swampy, meandering waterway that was the school's namesake. At recess some of us would head to the creek to see what we could find or what trouble we could get into in fifteen minutes. A favorite place to investigate was an old boathouse beside the creek, maybe a hundred yards from the schoolhouse. One day, it had been raining all morning, but the sun beamed brilliantly by early afternoon. Along with my buddies Larry and Steve—equally savvy, seven-year-old marsh muckers—I dashed down to the boathouse during afternoon recess.

On such days in May, frogs and turtles were active or sunning themselves on lily pads or partially submerged logs. Snapping turtles, however, were seldom sunbathers, lurking instead in the shallows where they might ambush the unsuspecting. We knew that the shadows of the boathouse waters were a favored haunt. We had seen them there before—some Frisbee-sized.

You should also know that snappers of such proportions were considered a delicacy by many western Michiganders. That "seven flavors of meat" were arranged between those leathery shells was a popular conviction—though I believe that required a well-developed palate or a vivid imagination.

From the creek bank, the boathouse extended on piers into the water. One by one, we each slipped through the opening where a door had once been hinged. Crowding onto a narrow platform along the front wall, it took a few moments for our eyes to adjust to the dim interior. The weathered structure was open at the far end, where the creek's dark-green waters glided by. They eddied inside, filling the boathouse with a slithering floor of duckweed and creek scum. A central plank walkway once provided access to boats moored on either side. Other than a coil of oily rope and a long-handled fishing net that hung on the wooden structure's front wall, the faint smell of gasoline was the only evidence of the shack's past history.

I think it was Larry, the gangly one, who went first. A few steps onto the walkway, he abruptly halted. "Snapper," he said in a hushed but urgent voice. Halfway into the boathouse, a black head the size of a tennis ball poked from the water—suspended there, as was our own momentary lapse in breathing. I reached for the net and passed it to Steve, who handed it to Larry. With one swift swoop, the beast was miraculously thrashing inside.

Caught off guard by the lurching reptile's power, Larry nearly went for a swim with the turtle. But Steve, who would become a sports hero in high school, grabbed the back of his shirt and steadied him just in time. Then all three of us latched on to the net's long handle. We struggled to drag it to the platform without knocking each other off the skinny walkway. After several ungainly and failed attempts, we hoisted the net from the water and drug our prize out the doorway.

"Holy cow! Look at the size of him!" Steve exclaimed. This was the biggest snapper any of us had *ever* seen. It barely fit inside the rim of the widemouthed net intended for landing the lake's largest walleyed and northern pike. Now the tattered netting was being chomped and thrashed to ribbons by the monster's jaws and claws. But the fun was just beginning.

With claws raking the ground, it was all we could do to keep him from towing the net, and us, back to the water. We had to get him off the ground and do it without being slashed by his feet or snatched in his beak.

Someone had the bright idea that we should flip him out of the net. By now, adrenalin, not reason, had taken charge. In fact, we may as well do it ourselves, because the hole he was shredding in the twine netting would soon provide a gaping escape to freedom.

The plan was this: Steve and Larry would flip him out, and I'd swoop in behind and grab him by the tail. Wow! He didn't like that at all. Spinning himself around, his jaws snapped just short of my arm. I remembered the story someone had told about how a big snapper like this could crush a broomstick in its jaws. My arm wasn't much bigger. When Steve jumped in and tried to lift him, the head shot out from the shell, searching for some flesh to punish. Steve loosed his grip just in time, and the turtle's legs pumped into high gear. Our prize was motoring around the boathouse toward the refuge of Green Creek's waters.

We now knew that none of us had the strength to hold the beast at arm's length, beyond the reach of claws and jaws. So just before he made his watery escape, two of us grabbed his tail from opposite sides and hoisted him into the air. With half the weight to support, we could carry him in outstretched arms between us—as he flailed and snapped and hissed—but for only a minute or so before our strength was sapped.

By now, recess had long run out. Miss Heart (her name defied the discipline with which she had ruled her school for four decades) would be on the warpath. No doubt. We yelled to a student our teacher had sent to find us, "Tell Miss Heart we caught a big turtle." A noble excuse for our tardiness, we reasoned.

Shortly, the school emptied out. Every first and second grader ran to see the Green Creek monster. A chorus of shouts and squeals greeted the mighty captors. "Wow, look at that!" "You gotta be kiddin' me!" "Look, Rocky—it's bigger than your dog!"

From the boathouse we took turns, two at a time, hoisting the reptile by its tail and carrying it as far as our puny arms would allow. When two of us tired and he thudded to the ground, the snapper began clawing a hasty retreat. But an infectious excitement soon overcame the others' timidity, and our relief would swoop in and repeat the drill for a few more yards up the hill. Leading the escort the rest of the way, even Miss Heart beamed an admiring smile at her students' collaborative efforts.

At the schoolhouse, the turtle was still pedaling his legs and hissing displeasure. I'm not sure what we thought we'd do with him there, but Miss Heart had that covered. In the school's storage room was a metal washtub. It was just big enough to accommodate the snapper. Getting the hang of turtle hoisting, a couple of us dropped him into the tub. But whoa! The sides were too low to keep him from climbing out, and he quickly flipped the tub on its side. Across the slippery hardwood, he tried to get traction toward the open door. But Steve and Larry were after the fugitive as Miss Heart and I retrieved a square of old plywood from the storage room. After plopping the angry reptile back into the tub, we laid the plywood on top. Up the plywood surged as the Green Creek monster pushed from beneath. So I sat on top, quite pleased as my classmates chirped and clapped.

Over the years, details of that day have stayed with me—an encouraging sign even as my hair has fallen out, my face has furrowed, and the pace of my morning runs has flagged. But I'm no longer certain with whom the snapper traveled from the school to my home. At the time, my youngest sister was just an infant, so my mom wasn't working. I believe that it was she who provided taxi service for the snapper. I can easily picture her opening the trunk of her Chevy sedan and a couple of us boys hoisting the turtle inside. When we got to the house and popped the trunk's latch, the turtle let himself out. Larry and I prodded and pulled him into the garage.

With my parents having passed on many years ago, I choose to remember the story this way, knitting that image of my mom ferrying the turtle into the rest of the story's sharper details. As such, this was one of those rare times that a boy later brags about his mother. An endearing instant that lasts a lifetime.

At the house, a small crowd of kids and parents soon gathered. Word of the giant snapper's capture had already spread, like any momentous event in rural Michigan. A length of rope was looped around his tail, and the turtle was suspended from a spring-loaded scale. The scale's needle danced up and down and then settled as everyone gawked in amazement. At twenty-four pounds, he was easily the largest snapper anyone could recall.

No one asked what would become of him. We lived in a time and place where most everyone knew. Larry's family, our next-door neighbors, the Dykstras, were the acknowledged hunter-gatherer clan in a neighborhood where most everyone enjoyed catching fish, picking wild berries and mushrooms, and hunting small game each fall. And Mrs. Dykstra was considered the best cook of game meat of anyone around. So that weekend, the Dykstras hosted a neighborhood dinner of roast turtle with all the trimmings (though I'm fuzzy on what trimmings complement roast snapper). On a platter at the center was a sweet-smelling spread of meat that made my mouth water. But try as I did to savor each bite of neck and back and leg muscles, to me it all just tasted like chicken.

THREE

THE WAY WEST

> There is always one moment in childhood
> when the door opens and lets the future in.
> —Graham Greene, *The Power and Glory*

My great-uncle Len gave me a split-cane fly rod when I was ten or eleven years old. He once used that pretty four-piece rod to entice brook trout and bass to strike colorful concoctions of fur and feather on western Michigan's lakes and streams. He had built a successful printing business in Grand Rapids, but his avocation was outdoor recreation, particularly fishing. Then he suffered a series of debilitating strokes—the first, shortly before I was born. My earliest memories were of him unsteadily shuffling with a cane. His illness progressed over seventeen years. Eventually, he was bedridden and unable to speak. Although disease ravaged his body, it didn't break his kind, selfless spirit or his passion for the outdoors.

I fondly recall the times I spent at the summer home of Uncle Len and my Aunt Irene. A wooden stairway of 360 steps wound from the gingerbread cottage in the woods down a precipitous embankment to the sandy beach of Lake Michigan far below. There were two little decks with benches for resting along the way. My sisters, Norma and Sandy, and I would sometimes race both down and back up the stairway, to and from the beach. I would have stayed longer than weekend visits, if I could have, exploring beaches and dunes, listening to dinner talk of politics and business and past days on the Big Lake, and seeing the devotion in their eyes.

♠

I was the first among the neighborhood kids to cast a fly to bluegills and bass on the lake behind our house. When I began fishing, everyone used cane poles with black casting line and hook tied onto the end—no reel to confuse the process of lobbing worms onto water. This was after my parents moved to the north shore of Muskegon Lake when I was seven. By age nine or ten, I and most other kids owned one of those fancy spinning outfits with a Johnson or Shakespeare reel. Few ever adopted, for lack of money or a caring uncle's interest, fly casting gear.

I felt self-conscious—I suppose even elitist in fly-fishing vernacular—standing on the middle seat of our family's twelve-foot wooden rowboat, working a seven-weight fly line and popper toward a wall of cattails. Without any guidance on proper casting technique, I suspect I was the butt of much snickering and joking, though I really don't recall.

I didn't know at the time when he gave it to me, but that fly rod represented more than the legacy of Uncle Len's joy in the sport. In truth, fly-fishing contributed to my decision to finish my college degree somewhere in the West. West meant anywhere beyond eastern Wisconsin where my cousins lived, which was the farthest west I'd ever been. For most working-class families I knew growing up in the 1950s and '60s, vacations outside Michigan—certainly beyond adjacent states—were extravagances. The West was still frontier, a great open space of cowboys and cattle and resplendent wild animals, a realm only recently invaded by *Sports Afield* photographers. Their glossy images of glistening trout plucked from cascading streams amid snow-capped peaks set my mind swirling. It all beguiled me like a Greek siren's song.

During my sophomore year at the local community college came a defining moment. Scrutinizing every university catalogue in the college's library, I compiled a list of the seventy-two universities that offered degrees in wildlife biology or wildlife management. I pared the list down to three schools, a task itself deserving of college credit.

Curricula, facilities, and important-sounding faculty bios were all discriminating factors. Equally important was the physical environment of each institution . . . things like proximity to mountains; wilderness areas; and, of course, trout streams. The qualifiers were Northern Arizona University in Flagstaff, Oregon State University in Corvallis, and the University of Montana in Missoula.

To reach a final decision, I proposed a road trip to my chemistry lab partner, Ed. His reddish-blond Dennis the Menace hair, twinkling eyes, and boyish round face signaled that unattended items were fair game for his Bunsen burner. A perfect cross-country traveling companion.

"We could head west on Saturday morning," I prodded shortly before the upcoming spring break.

Ed was as travel challenged as I was, and equally keen on a western adventure. Without much discussion of why we shouldn't do it, we began poring over a road map. We'd take Interstate 94 into Montana; check out Missoula for a day; and continue on to Corvallis, to Flagstaff, and back to Michigan the following weekend. Only one problem . . . I was apprehensive that my parents would veto the trip. After presenting them with this grand idea, my dad approached me the next day.

"Okay, your mom and I have talked it over," he began. I felt myself tighten in preparation for what was to follow. "If you're set on doing this, you can go."

As my anxiety melted into elation, he added, "But there are two conditions. We expect you to call us along the way. And I want you to take my car."

He was right. My Ford wasn't up to the task.

I now think the adventure was his as well as my own, if only vicariously. My dad was taken by the West, though like me, he'd never been there. *Gunsmoke, Rawhide,* and other western TV shows and movies were his kind of entertainment. After I returned, he proudly wore the cowboy hat I bought him in Montana, in those days a sight in Muskegon nearly as rare as a palm tree.

So off Ed and I drove that March morning in Dad's sky-blue Oldsmobile 98. We made Missoula in three days. It helped that Montana's posted speed limit on the interstate in those days was "Reasonable and Prudent." A teenager's dream! Still, three days was remarkable, considering that much of I-94 in Montana was two lanes in 1968. One stretch was gravel. Plus, there was so much to see and photograph along the way: mounted cowboys and their dogs moving cattle; skittering pronghorn antelope and big-eared mule deer; soaring mountains and snaking streams; a stockyard sign advertising "Used Cows"; and birds that I'd never seen . . . extravagant magpies and crested Steller's jays. Although Ed was drawn more to the physical sciences, buying a nature field guide became a necessity for us both.

The un-Michigan-like geology we glimpsed from the highway was a mesmerizing magnet to Ed. We couldn't resist stops at alluring landmarks, like Theodore Roosevelt National Park. For my part, Roosevelt, I'd read, was a preeminent figure in American conservation. If this multihued jumble of buttes, badlands, and valleys was named in that great man's honor, how could I not second Ed? Teddy's monument was a must see!

With no travel guide beyond our Rand-McNally, we anticipated with wild imaginations what next lay ahead. What color were the Yellowstone River's waters? How grand the view from the Continental Divide? And would we be overrun by wildlife when we refueled in Deer Lodge?

We arrived in Missoula on Monday night. As on the previous evenings, we each called home from our motel room. Collect, of course. After reassuring my dad that the car and I were alright, I regaled him with adjective-laced descriptions of the "real mountains" we finally drove through. I couldn't help but detect some envy (or was it sadness?) in his voice. Except for his tour of the South Pacific in World War II, neither he nor my mom had traveled much, certainly not "out West."

Dad had left high school to join the U.S. Marines. And after she graduated high school, my mom went straight to her first bookkeeping job. Like so many returning servicemen on the heels of the war, they married and started a family, beginning with me. Their days were fully duty bound, paying the bills and raising three kids.

My future after high school wasn't something we had talked about much. Given my love of learning, perhaps my parents considered college a foregone conclusion. Now here Ed and I were—two thousand miles from home on my road to tomorrow. Next stop, the University of Montana!

⚹

The next morning after breakfast, we drove with great anticipation to the U of M campus. No bustle of students and briefcase-toting professors. We found it all but deserted.

"What's the enrollment here?" Ed asked as we hoofed our way toward Old Main, the administrative office indicated on the campus map I'd been mailed.

"About eight thousand, I think."

"People or bears?" Ed teased as we walked past an eight-foot bronze of a grizzly bear.

Old Main's portico opened into a high-ceilinged foyer. Impressive renderings of people I assumed were important in the school's history adorned buff walls accented by russet wood trim. Seeing no one to ask for directions to the admissions office, I entered the open door to my left. It was a large receiving office, I surmised, with a rank of oak file cabinets and two chairs for guests with business. But no one sat behind the broad wooden desk.

A door to an adjoining office stood ajar. I whispered to Ed, "I'm going to peek inside."

Gazing around the receiving office, he said, "I'll wait here."

I stepped through the door into a larger room. A distinguished-looking gentleman, dressed in suit and tie, looked up from a stack of papers organized on an imposing desk. He asked, "May I help you?"

I blurted out, "I'm Bruce Smith from Michigan, and I'm here to learn more about the University of Montana."

He looked me over and replied, "Well, Mr. Smith, I'm the University president. I may be able to help you with that," and then added, leaning forward in his chair, "seeing that my secretary has apparently stepped out."

It was one of those omigod moments when naïveté meets reality. After apologizing for bursting into his office, I gushed the whole story of how I had compiled a list of seventy-two universities that offered wildlife degrees, how I had narrowed it down with his university among the top three (smile and raised eyebrows from the president), how my friend (wave to Ed to come meet the president) and I drove out on spring break, blah, blah, blah.

He nodded and kindly acknowledged our considerable efforts to learn more about the University of Montana, the oldest institution of higher learning in the state of Montana. He added, "This week's spring break here also."

How stupid of me, I thought. Of course, many schools must schedule spring break the same week as does Muskegon County Community College.

Reading my awkwardness and without delay, he picked up the telephone receiver and dialed. "Phil, Bob Pantzer here. I have two young men who drove all the way here from Michigan to learn about the university's wildlife biology program. If it wouldn't be an imposition, could you drive down and show them some of our facilities."

Twenty minutes later, Dr. P. L. Wright introduced himself to us as the chairman of the wildlife biology program and then whisked us off to the Health Sciences Building. During the walk to the four-story, brick building, Dr. Wright regaled us with details of the wildlife program's history and some of its eminent faculty, including Dr. John J. Craighead (most famous for the pioneering grizzly bear studies he and his twin brother Frank were conducting in Yellowstone National Park). Then we got the grand tour. It concluded with a mesmerizing walk through the museum that housed study skins, skulls, and pickled embryos of mammals and birds. Specimens ranged from a gigantic grizzly bear hide draped across one wall to tiny stuffed hummingbirds arranged in rows in one of dozens of slide-out metal collection drawers. For me, it was a delectable feast for the eyes.

"This is a black-footed ferret, rarest mammal in North America," he said, supporting in outstretched palms the cotton-stuffed skin of an overgrown weasel. "I found it in eastern Montana in 1939, driving from Wisconsin to Missoula," he continued with genuine enthusiasm to share the story. "I had finished my doctorate degree and was on my way to my first job . . . the only one I've ever had!" he said with a toothy grin.

"Was it alive?" I asked, wondering if he had started his career by bumping off one of a vanishing breed of animals.

"Oh no," he replied, settling the tawny skin with black mask, legs, and tail tip onto the vacant drawer space. "It was dead. I spotted it at fifty miles per hour on the roadside," he laughed, thoroughly pleased with himself.

"So you picked it up and brought it with you," Ed responded, ever the keen observer.

"Well, not quite that easily," Dr. Wright shot him a wry smile. "After I pulled to the roadside and examined it, I had a choice to make. You see, it was a hot August day. Added to the foul smell of its anal scent glands, the ferret was already ripe. But still in good condition, mind you. No maggots yet, and the hair hadn't begun to slip."

"So what was the choice you had to make?" I pressed him.

"To leave it or take it, of course. You see, my wife was waiting patiently in the car. We were newlyweds," his eyes beamed. "It was another five hundred miles to Missoula. I looked at the ferret, then looked at the Model A. It had no trunk like modern cars. I was torn. I could risk losing my new bride if I brought it along. On the other hand, what a prize specimen for the new mammalogist to arrive with!"

His grin broadened, creasing his cheeks, "I couldn't just leave it there for the ravens! My wife still tells people that I chose a dead ferret over her." And all three of us burst into laughter.

Locking the door on the museum's treasures, this engaging man escorted us down the stairs to the first-floor exit. In the brisk March air, Dr. P. L. Wright enumerated ongoing research projects of the wildlife department's professors and students. "We've got students studying reproduction of golden eagles, biology of trumpeter swans, polar bear behavior at Hudson Bay, coyote and bobcat predation, how logging affects elk habitat and hunting . . . oh, and of course John Craighead's studies of Yellowstone's grizzlies and elk. Anyway, what are your impressions of the university?"

With my head spinning from this gracious reception, I gushed, "This is great. Just what I'm looking for." If I hadn't known before, I did now. Ed and I thanked him profusely for taking the time to personally show us around. Then we chattered our way back toward the Oldsmobile.

"Did you see the size of that bear skin?" Ed demanded, as if we'd just witnessed the premier of *King Kong.*

"Yeah, unbelievable. And that ferret story!" I responded, reviewing the details.

I vividly recall that morning and warmly reflect on how such encounters can shape one's life. Six years later I would be a graduate student, teaching the mammalogy lab for Dr. Wright, by then a renowned scientist nationally and a legend in Montana.

⁂

I don't recall what Ed and I did the rest of that day. I do know that by day's end I'd made a decision. "Hey, Dad," I blurted when I called him that night. "We're going to be home early."

"What happened?" he answered with understandable concern.

"Don't worry. Everything's okay. But there's no need for Ed and me to go to Oregon or Arizona. I've decided already. I'm going to enroll here in Missoula, at the home of the University of Montana Grizzlies!"

Ed was okay with changing our plans. Although we both wanted to see the big forests of Oregon, the Pacific Ocean, and Arizona's desert, it was already Wednesday. Making it to Corvallis and Flagstaff and back home on Sunday would've been grueling, probably impossible. So instead, we hung out in Missoula another day, visiting the campus again to see the sports facilities, the student union, and most everything else that remained open during spring break. Missoula itself had much to offer: sporting-goods stores, historic buildings housing western art and collectibles, the landmark Wilma and Roxy theaters, and a couple of cool beer joints. Besides, Missoula was situated in a beautiful valley. The surrounding mountains—real mountains, not the high spots called mountains in the Midwest—gave rise to storied trout waters: the Blackfoot, the Bitterroot, and the Clark Fork of the Columbia. I already pictured myself living here . . . a sure enough Montanan!

Time was no longer an issue. So Ed and I rerouted our return to see the world's first national park. We checked the highway map. At Exit 298 near Bozeman, I wheeled the big Oldsmobile off the freeway. On a course due south, Highway 191 passed through sparsely inhabited ranchland, land on which today the cattle are largely replaced by billboards and exurban sprawl. After fifteen miles, the two-lane entered Gallatin Canyon, a narrow cut through sedimentary ramparts where I later learned that bighorn sheep foraged in winter. Maybe we just missed their buffy coats against the tan-blotched background of snow and rock. But we saw none. I was probably too focused on the icy blacktop and stealing glances at the rushing waters of the Gallatin River that paralleled the road.

After winding through thirty miles of pristine landscape, the canyon widened. Stringers of Douglas fir and lodgepole pine wove left and right. They garnished ridges and swales blanketed by two or more feet of shimmering white. Tawny ribbons of grass showed only where winds had lashed and swept the more severe exposures.

Ed pointed to a thin line of animals on the horizon, darkly silhouetted against a brooding cloud bank. Even through binoculars, we weren't sure what they were. I remember thinking that their necks seemed longer than Midwest whitetails. In retrospect, they were the first elk either of us had ever seen. At the time, they were just food for speculation. We drove on as they vanished beyond the ridge.

Another twenty miles and we spotted a small brown sign barely poised above the roadside snowbank. Etched in pale-yellow lettering, it proclaimed, "Yellowstone National Park." My heart leaped. We were in Yellowstone!

A cloak of untracked snow smothered all but sporadic glimpses of the Gallatin. Clumps of willow stems delimited its course with maroon, lavender, and yellow-green splotches. Farther on, a sliver of water opened maybe one hundred yards left of the roadway. I steered the car to the roadside, where a wall of snow blocked Ed's view of all but the sky.

"Nice spot for a stroll," Ed quipped. He knew what I was up to.

I explained days earlier that the two fishing rods in the trunk were destined to test some western river for wild trout. I didn't know then that Yellowstone was a possibility. My congenial companion and I had shared a great adventure so far. Now he cast me one of those "you've gotta be kiddin' me" glances, surely thinking that skiing would have been a better choice of sport.

"I've got two rods. Do you want to give it a try?" I asked.

"Thanks, but I'll just watch from the warmth of the car." Ed's grin revealed that he intended to fully enjoy my apparent lapse of sanity.

"You sure?" I pressed, as I stepped onto snow-packed pavement and felt the frigid air bite my face.

With a definitive nod he affirmed, "Oh yeah, I'm sure. Say 'hi' to the fishies for me."

I shuffled cautiously beside the car and opened its yawning trunk. I fondly eyed the case with the pretty split bamboo inside. Uncle Len would be so pleased to see me working the green fly line in tight loops over Yellowstone waters. Squinting across the snowscape, I thought better. I reluctantly extracted the spinning rod and reel and a small box of brightly colored lures. This would have to do. If the fishing were fast, I'd return for the fly rod.

I tugged on a stocking cap and wool gloves. With a quick reconnoiter of my destination, I kicked steps to scale the roadside berm of snow. Once on top, I only sunk to the rim of my knee-high rubber boots. However, beyond where the snow had been showered by snowplows, I quickly found myself postholing with each step, above my knees . . . sporadically even crotch-deep. *Plunge one foot in, extract the other, repeat.* I glanced back at the Olds. Ed was enjoying this.

Soon my hair was soaked. Rivulets of sweat trickled down my back, despite the subfreezing temperature. My breathing surged in clouds of steam, like that of the horses we'd seen frolicking in a pasture that morning. No matter, I was undeterred.

As I felt the snow, now packed around my lower blue jean legs, melting into my boots, I reached my destination. An ice shelf guarded a rollicking frenzy of water that tumbled over rocks and dodged beneath the snow-laden ice again. I had maybe forty yards of open water to test and, based on my Midwest experience, not a likely spot to hold a fish. Discouraged? Not at all. I was in Yellowstone Park to catch trout, and catch trout I would try. I had the whole place to myself. Imagine that!

I began casting a silver spinner, a few tosses in the near riffle and then a few more behind a glazed rock upstream. I felt the current tug the lure along, threatening to suck it beneath the ice. All the while, the smile never left my face. Maybe it was frozen in place.

I don't recall how long I fished. The dancing water and rhythm of the casting suspended time. Maybe twenty or thirty minutes had elapsed, including interludes to pinch ice from the spinning rod's guides, when I realized my pants had frozen solid. I retrieved the lure a last time and turned away from the Gallatin. In a Frankenstein stagger, I regained partial articulation of my knee joints and retraced my steps to the road . . . *plunge-extract, plunge-extract.* At least the postholes were already set.

I lurched in frozen socks on unfeeling feet. Clumps of snow and shards of ice cascaded off my jeans. When I poked my head in the driver's side window, which Ed had opened, he roared, "Catch any?"

Not funny, I thought, now uncontrollably shivering. Resisting a sarcastic reply, I chattered, "No-o-o, but the fishing was great!"

As fast as I could, I changed clothes next to the car. Southbound on Highway 191 again, Ed recounted how he had nearly made himself sick laughing. Mocking my Frankenstein stagger from behind the wheel, he drove and entertained himself while I continued to rub my painfully thawing feet.

"I'm so cold, master," he bantered. "I only walk this way because my pants are frozen!" And some other stuff I've since forgotten. But as sensation returned to my extremities, I was self-satisfied and not the least defeated. *I had fished for trout in Yellowstone!*

We drove on to snowbound West Yellowstone, the gateway town at the park's west entrance. We learned that Yellowstone's roads were snowed shut and closed for the winter to motor vehicles—except snow machines of course. That somehow hadn't occurred to us. Roads didn't take time off in Michigan. This was the end of the line. So we grabbed a bite to eat, turned the Olds around, and headed back north on 191.

As we began the long drive back to Muskegon, tragic news immediately assailed us. Traveling down the Gallatin Valley toward a motel somewhere in central Montana, we switched on the car's radio. Dr. Martin Luther King had been assassinated!

In late March 1968, Dr. King went to Memphis, Tennessee, to show support for the striking sanitary public workers' union. On April 3, he addressed a rally, delivering his "I've Been to the Mountaintop" speech at Mason Temple. Standing on the second-floor balcony of his room in the Lorraine Motel, King was shot and killed at 6:01 p.m. the next day. The assassination led to nationwide rioting in more than sixty cities. Our return to Michigan took us through Chicago just two days after the assassination. King and his followers had demonstrated there, including marches in 1966 and 1967. I still can see the gangs of angry young men with clubs, chains, and tire irons roaming the not-so-freeway we navigated through Cicero. Battered, disabled, and abandoned cars littered the route. More than once, rioters all but blocked our path. We just kept telling each other, "Keep moving. We've gotta keep moving!"

When President Johnson finally declared a national day of mourning, the rioting had rampaged unabated for five days. Our close call in Chicago searingly demonstrated how troubled

America was during that time of social change and the Vietnam War. We were glued to the newscasts while driving north through Michigan. I recall telling Ed, when we finally saw the city-limit sign, "I've never been this happy to be in Muskegon."

🌲

Nearly three years later, I again drove west on I-94 . . . this time, alone. The car was a new 1970 Pontiac Firebird, a present to myself upon my return from Vietnam.

My path had taken an abrupt turn. I'd opted not to enroll at the University of Montana in 1968—the year two of my high school buddies spilled their blood on Vietnamese soil. Ray was killed near the end of his tour with the U.S. Army. Barely a month in country, Jerry, a marine who was newly married, lost his life just south of the DMZ.

Following my sophomore year of college, on a sticky August afternoon in 1968, I walked into a Marine Corps recruiting office and unceremoniously signed my name. My two-year enlistment guaranteed I'd be a combat marine after five months of training. I spent the next year as a squad leader, carrying an M60 machine gun through the jungles and rice paddies of South Vietnam.

That decision wasn't wholly service driven. I was financially struggling and burned out. I'd worked full time each summer and twenty-five hours a week while a full-time student. I reasoned that the GI Bill would help me finish my degree in Montana without the burden of student loans to cover out-of-state tuition. This was time-honored wisdom of a child whose parents were children of the Great Depression era. "Don't buy what you can't afford."

It was years after the drumbeat of protest demonstrations and the songs of antiwar activists had faded that I came to terms with the folly of Vietnam. I was but one of 2.6 million who served and one of the 300,000 who were wounded in a war that served no purpose, tore our country apart at home, and left its warriors feeling disenfranchised upon returning home. Yet I consider myself one of the fortunate. My shrapnel wounds were not severe. I was not among the fifty-eight thousand who sacrificed their lives, ostensibly for ideological and political motives—not for our nation's security, as we were led to believe.

After working most of the next year to stash money for tuition, I embarked on a lifetime adventure. This anticipated chapter of my life was part of what kept me going through the insanity and ugliness of Vietnam and its stark contrast to the order and beauty of the natural world of my adolescence.

If a year in combat did anything for me, it helped me discover at an early age how fragile life is and how important it is to do something of value with our time on Earth. Conserving the natural heritage of my homeland seemed a worthy enough cause. En route, immersing myself in the West's wildlands was my path to reconciliation and to leaving the war behind.

Now, it was early New Year's Day morning 1971. With the aftertaste of celebration in my mouth, I was cruising back to Missoula beneath a star-spangled sky. Despite my excitement, I had no idea what adventures awaited me in the Rocky Mountain West.

FOUR

THE DEER HUNT

No man has a good enough memory to be a successful liar.
—Abraham Lincoln

Ron Ness was a fellow student at the University of Montana in Missoula. A stout, dark-haired Norwegian, he hailed from Owatonna, Minnesota—heartland of the frozen north. We became friends and fishing buddies in 1972 when I met him in a silviculture class, or maybe it was forest ecology. He introduced me to fellow Minnesotans and forestry majors Ben and Chuck. We were each putting ourselves through college on savings from summer work and part-time jobs after classes. I had the additional backing of the GI Bill.

At the time, we all lived on campus, but we soon hatched a plan to escape from dorm life. We found our little utopia—a musty-smelling, cement block–walled vault in the basement of an ancient bungalow, just eight blocks from campus. It had the basics . . . refrigerator and stove, bathroom, two sets of bunk beds (yes, bunk beds!), a couple of old wooden desks, and a nineteen-inch black-and-white TV one of us brought along. Most importantly, splitting the 175-dollar monthly rent (including utilities) made life off campus autonomous and affordable.

We were all hunters, to varying degrees. Like so many other kids of the rural Midwest, we each graduated from BB guns to shotguns at age twelve, when we could legally hunt small game—squirrels, ducks, and upland game birds. I owned rabbit hounds, beagles, from my early teens and became obsessed with hunting cottontails and snowshoe hares with the neighborhood kids in western Michigan.

It was my dad who introduced me to hunting. After claiming my first victim, a woodcock, I was hooked on the joy and challenge of the sport. The woodcock's a probing-billed bird of deciduous woodlands, resembling its close relative the common snipe. It feeds on insects and earthworms that inhabit damp litter and soil of the forest floor. When disturbed, it bursts through the trees in dizzying, corkscrew pirouettes. When my dad and I flushed that single bird, the 410-gauge shotgun came instinctively to my shoulder as he'd trained me to practice. The woodcock was killed and simultaneously cleaned. In hunting jargon, I "patterned the target."

I picked up the pathetic-looking creature about fifteen yards from where I had fired and acknowledged, "I probably should have let it get out there a little farther."

Dad broke into a proud smile and nodded something like, "Next time, Son."

🌲

Ron, Ben, Chuck, and I had planned a mule deer hunt that fall of 1972. We settled on Rogers Pass, near the headwaters of Montana's famed Blackfoot River, made famous in the 1992 film *A River Runs through It*, based on Norman Maclean's novella of the same name.

Rogers Pass may best be known as the site of the coldest temperature ever recorded in the United States outside Alaska—minus seventy degrees Fahrenheit in 1954. Like all mountain passes in the northern Rockies, Rogers is a snow catcher. As the prevailing westerly flow forces moisture-laden air up mountain slopes, a phenomenon called adiabatic cooling compresses the air. That reduces its ability to hold the same amount of moisture as when the air is warmer. Precipitation falls as snow—sometimes lots of it—when temperatures are cold enough. For every one thousand feet of elevation gained, air temperature cools by roughly three degrees Fahrenheit, depending on its relative humidity. This is called the adiabatic lapse rate, although you seldom hear the term used, even by folks living in the Rockies. But everyone knows that it gets colder as you go up.

As I recall, neither of these facts regarding weather conditions had any bearing on the selection of our hunting site. I say this because the best hunting vehicle any of us owned was an old station wagon with rear-wheel drive.

From the time we left Missoula after classes on Friday, until we arrived at what seemed a good site to pitch a tent in a clearing beside a logging road, we had gained more than three thousand feet of elevation. Despite a brooding Montana sky and subfreezing temperatures, a dusting of snow promised ideal conditions for tracking and stalking deer, we agreed.

Vivid details remain from that deer hunt on Rogers Pass with my three college buddies. The first is the harvesting of my first big game animal. Ben and Chuck had each been successful the first day we hunted. We all pitched in to drag those two deer back to our campsite in the accumulating snow, now several inches deep following a steady snowfall overnight. But who harvested what didn't really matter. This was hunting in the primal hunter-gatherer tradition, with camaraderie and the sharing of protein the only goals of the adventure.

Fresh tracks had been plentiful on Sunday, but I had been unable to glimpse or track down an animal and was getting discouraged. Then, as I trudged back toward camp late that morning, I spotted a large doe in a woodland. Just a half mile from our tents, the doe was feeding in a thicket of ivory-trunked aspen and a scattering of pines. When I spotted her, she simultaneously locked eyes with mine. She hesitated too long.

The bullet from the German 8 mm Mauser rifle—the one my dad gave me when I left Michigan for Montana—dropped her where she had stood. It was only as I approached to dress her that I noticed two fawns hanging back farther in the trees. I felt the air go out of me. *They must belong to her.* One look at her swollen mammary glands confirmed my fears.

This was the first large mammal I'd ever killed. But I had no intention of orphaning fawns. I had told myself before hunting season began that I would only shoot a buck, or a doe that wasn't accompanied by fawns. There was no scientific basis for my decision, no legal requirement, only an emotional one . . . a personal imperative. I believe it was an ethical outgrowth of lessons learned from my father and grandfather in Michigan's woodlands and cedar swamps. "Follow the game laws." "Only shoot what you plan to eat." "Respect all living things." And at that time, to encourage the growth of Michigan's whitetail population, most deer hunting was restricted to bucks—a holdover following the collapse of the state's deer population during the 1940s and 1950s.

I found myself trembling, wishing I'd hesitated and scanned the surrounding trees more carefully, just a little longer before squeezing the trigger. The fawns may have been hidden from view, but that possibility didn't relieve my distress.

I lingered on these thoughts awhile longer, reliving the event and my feelings about it. Then I tagged and dressed the deer.

There is a poignant reality to being a meat eater that hunters experience but is largely lost on those who purchase their table fare at a store. The steaks in Safeway don't have soft brown eyes or fur. Yet prepackaged sirloins were once the muscles of living, breathing creatures, too. They're just aesthetically presented as packaged products to carnivorous consumers—pleasantly lighted, cleaned of hair, and chilled to avoid the sight of oozing blood. Never mind that the living conditions of poultry, cattle, and swine are far less wholesome than that of wildlife roaming wildlands. Or that, by design, the lone reason for the existence of a Rhode Island Red or Black Angus is to produce protein for people. Or that much of the land on which domestic stock are raised—and, for that matter, on which grains, fruits, and vegetables are produced—was once wildland with far greater capacity to produce diverse communities of plants and animals than its converted, agricultural state can sustain. Indeed, much of the credit for conservation of North America's wild places and vital natural habitats is owed to hunters and other devoted wildlife constituencies. Better than most, they have understood that diverse and healthy landscapes sustain wildlife populations, which among other ecological services and pleasures provide renewable food resources to us.

Yet we know from aboriginal cultures that ancient hunter-gatherers, too, were conflicted about the taking of life to sustain their own. They honored, even worshiped, animal spirits while eating their flesh. Native Americans saw all living things as their relations yet harvested what they needed. I've known modern hunters, too, who recognize as gifts the surplus they harvest from our wildlands. As Ted Kerasote eloquently penned in his book, *Blood Ties*,

> The elk who live in these forests, the blueberries who grow in its understory, the streamside lettuce I put in my salads can't be grown by anyone. True, blueberries are cultivated, and elk are ranched in many places, but they aren't the same blueberries and elk as these wild ones, though they may bear the same genetic makeup. Wild elk, along with all the other creatures and plants of nature, are what the earth still provides from her initial grace. They can't be planted or harvested or ranched; they can only be received. Whether the means of receiving them is a spear, a gun, or one's plucking fingers matters less than the state of mind moving hands to action.

As I dressed out the doe, a sense of all of this swelled in my gut. Over time I'd come to grasp it with greater clarity, granting intellectual allowance for my active role in the food chain. I, human, remained a predator, living out a multimillion-years-old drama of my ancestors. The raison d'être, however, made taking the doe's life no less significant a matter. The initial emotion of ending her life lingered, and I felt content that it did.

♠

When next I looked up, the fawns had vanished. It was late October. They were nearly weaned and would find their way to winter grounds, I told myself, as these social animals do. The way back to camp was mostly uphill. I chose to drag the doe there on my own through eight inches of powdery snow. I wanted the solitude, to dwell on my thoughts and feelings and to complete the task of harvesting on my own—to *earn this protein* as I would come to internalize it during future hunts. Dressed out, she weighed one hundred pounds or less; and although my sweat ran freely in the chill air, the physical exertion was rewarding.

At camp, I was greeted by the enthusiastic congratulations that make communal hunting so rewarding. After sketching the details of my morning—the route I had hunted and how I came upon the deer—we hung the doe from the limb of a large Douglas fir tree, near those that Chuck and Ben had taken. I kept my regrets about taking the doe's life to myself, not knowing how the others might react to my feelings of guilt.

The second vivid memory of the Rogers Pass hunt is Ron's deer. Ron alone had not harvested an animal yet on Sunday, the day we planned to break camp to make Monday-morning classes at the U. The other option was to pack everything up Monday morning and leave well before daylight, for the two-hour drive back to Missoula. To this suggestion, someone offered that he'd rather be poked in the eye with a stick. Besides, it was still snowing. We were basically out of food. And the tires on the soon-to-be deer transport had seen their better days. The station wagon would be loaded with camping gear, three deer, and the four of us. I could almost hear the suspension groan. Plowing through nearly a foot of snow was not the design purpose of this Ford.

So it was agreed. We'd begin packing up soon after a hearty lunch of anything we could find left in the Coleman cooler. We'd head out before nightfall.

Ron had been somewhat subdued since my return. Until our departure deliberations ended, he'd mostly poked at the fire's embers with a stick and occasionally nodded in concurrence with what was being said. Now he piped up, "Were there any other deer with the doe you got?"

That was the question I did not want to hear. I paused, considering my options. I could say, "No." No one would question it. But reflexively, out came the truth. "After I shot her, I saw two fawns that were probably hers. I didn't know they were there when I shot." And after another pause, I added, "I didn't see any other does."

No one spoke, but I assumed each was recalling what I'd said on Friday's drive from Missoula. This was my first big game hunt. I would shoot only a buck or doe without fawns or nothing at all. Perhaps the others didn't remember my exact words, but I heard them ricocheting inside my head.

Following a pensive furrowing of the brow, Ron asked for details about where the fawns were. Chuck, Ron's constant conscience and needler-in-chief, drawled something like, "You aren't really thinking of . . ."

A sheepish grin crossed Ron's face. "I'll just take a stroll down that way," he interrupted while shouldering his rifle. "Won't be gone long."

The obligatory comments were exchanged after Ron's departure. Things like, "Can you believe that?" "Only Ron would go after a fawn." And, "If he gets one, at least he won't need any help getting it back to camp!" Just your typical derisive remarks swapped among friends.

Not thirty minutes had passed when we heard the report of a rifle in the direction Ron set out. Then a second shot, followed by a third. Then silence. In the midst of our packing, we looked from one face to another. A few speculative hypotheses were exchanged. Crossing my mind was a Native American saying I first heard in my youth, "First shot meat, second shot maybe, third shot no meat."

"Well, what happened?" Chuck grinned when Ron trudged into camp.

Ron struggled to make eye contact, kicked a stick of firewood, and forced a grin himself. "I missed."

"Missed what?" Chuck shot back. "You missed a fawn?"

Ron stretched his neck, padded aimlessly around, and found a seat on a cut log by the campfire, where coffee simmered in a blackened pot. "Yeah, I missed a fawn . . . three times."

Laughter roared among us. Chuck amiably chided his friend that this was the first case of fawn fever he had ever heard of. Thereafter, "fawn fever" became part of our lexicon, freely invoked whenever Ron got a little too puffed up about anything.

🌲

The trip down the snow-blanketed logging road to its junction with Highway 200 was nothing short of harrowing. Thankfully, another vehicle had broken tracks, and the route was mostly downhill. Even a moderate incline would have likely proven an impossible challenge for the Ford.

About sundown, we rolled into Missoula, where even in the early 1970s a station wagon with three deer strapped on the roof was a sight to behold. Pedestrians stared and pointed. Oncoming cars slowed, and heads turned to take a look. We made a beeline for our place. After a hasty stop to hang the deer in the landlord's garage, we headed out for celebratory pizzas and beer.

I'd like to say that the four of us hunted deer again. I would have enjoyed that. But before the next hunting season, Ben and Chuck graduated from the university and moved on to their careers. Ron and I had each found our own little rental utopias on opposite sides of town. But the two of us continued to share hunting and fishing adventures from time to time. During those days afield, he didn't bring up the doe I shot with fawns, and I didn't mention Ron's attack of fawn fever. Okay, maybe I did . . . just once or twice.

FIVE

THE ELK HUNT

Success is going from failure to failure
without losing your enthusiasm.
—Abraham Lincoln

From the bookcase headboard, the alarm clock blared like machine-gun fire, a sound all too familiar a few years earlier in my life. My hand wrestled around the clock, finally finding the kill button. Through the haze of half consciousness, my first sensation was the pressure in my head. And second, why was I awakened in what must be the middle of the night? As I caught myself falling back to sleep, I remembered . . . *This is the opening day of hunting season!*

I rose on one elbow to blearily verify the time . . . 5:00 a.m. The urge to call Ron nearly overcame me. *Maybe we should wait a couple of hours. The elk aren't going anywhere.*

Ron Ness and I had shared a basement apartment with two fellow students, Ben and Chuck, the year before. Now he lived across town in an apartment even smaller than mine. His was a cubicle above the Wilma Theatre on Higgins Street. Mine was a one-stall garage converted to an apartment, near the University of Montana's Dornblaser football field. It came complete with curbside parking, deficient heating, and insulation enough for Mississippi but hardly Montana. That's what you got for seventy dollars a month in 1973. I also got frozen bathroom pipes both winters I lived there. But that I had covered. An all-hours gas station was just a couple of blocks away.

Growing up during the 1950s and 1960s, I never hunted big game in Michigan, where white-tailed deer and black bear qualify as such. To this day, the state prides itself on the size of its whitetail bucks, even though a small herd (by western states standards) of eight hundred to nine hundred elk roam the Pigeon River country near Grayling—animals I neither hunted nor saw during my twenty years in the state.

Ron, on the other hand, had done a little deer hunting in Minnesota, though I don't recall him claiming he'd ever bagged one. Now we two Midwesterners were joined by common bond. We sought an animal more than twice the size of the biggest white-tailed deer either of us had ever seen. At five hundred pounds live weight, a mature cow elk would provide a year's supply of high-quality meat. And a bull could easily weigh two hundred pounds more. Of course we'd share the meat, because we'd share the work—the inevitable toil of getting the elk from forest to freezer.

As I tugged on my jeans from the edge of the bed, it occurred to me. Not all hunters prepare for their first elk hunt as Ron and I had done. The evening before, we joined friends at one of Missoula's finer dining establishments for burgers and beers. It was fifty-cent pitcher night, and evening soon became the next day. By the time I got home, it was nearly 1:00 a.m. Doing the math, I'd had four hours of sleep when the alarm announced that I had just half an hour to pick up Ron.

I finished dressing; gathered up my rifle, hunting knife, meat saw, rope, binoculars, and blaze-orange vest; and gulped down some cereal. Into my canvas rucksack, I stuffed the makings of lunch: a can of tuna (make that two cans), several slices of bread, a Hershey's bar, and an apple with a brown crater on one side—the four basic food groups, plus a canteen of water. I remembered a can opener at the last minute—a very good sign that I was now awake and ready for the day. Before leaving, I grabbed the aspirin bottle from the medicine cabinet, just in case Ron wasn't feeling chipper.

After climbing the interior stairs to his apartment, I rapped on the door. Ron apparently was not as far along in his preparations as I was. On the third try, I elicited a sound that was unmistakably a human attempting to speak: "Alright, alright. I'm coming!"

After Ron gathered himself, we were out the door and down the road in my Dodge pickup. The drive to our agreed-upon hunting spot took less than an hour. That's the beauty of a place like Missoula. Outstanding hunting, fishing, hiking, and rafting areas were all within a quarter tank of fuel for Old Blue.

The Dodge ground to a halt well after first light illuminated the finger-long needles and rusty bark of ponderosa pines. The chill air smelled of pine and fir and did wonders for our outlook on life. We were elk hunters. Sure enough. And we would find an elk. After all, I was a wildlife biology major, and Ron . . . well Ron was a forester.

We decided to split up to improve our chances of bumping into our quarry. The plan, as such, was "I'll go this way, and you go that way." When one of us got an elk, we'd signal the other with two quick rifle shots followed by another. I think we added a caveat that if neither of us were successful—an unimaginable outcome—we would meet back at the truck at such-and-such an hour. I downed two more aspirin, handed Ron the bottle, checked my compass, and melted into the forest.

After plodding for an hour up a steep spur ridge of the Sapphire Mountains, my efforts had yielded only sightings of scolding red squirrels, chattering chickadees, and a few croaking ravens that glided overhead. I found a flat, needle-laden spot at the base of a pine and plopped down. I rested my rifle on the rucksack beside me and eased back against the tree's welcoming trunk. With the sun warm on my face, I thought it good strategy to sit quietly and listen and watch for a while. The forest floor was dry, and I could only imagine how much more easily an elk could hear me than the reverse. That was my logic. But lack of sleep and the effect of alcohol dehydration probably closed the deal.

It's possible this was a good spot to detect an elk. It's also possible that one or more passed by while I was propped against that tree. Instead, I only dreamed of how I would hold the crosshairs of my four-power scope behind the shoulder of one of those great animals and how I'd relish signaling Ron that I'd actually pulled off what we'd talked about all summer.

Maybe most of all, I fancied a locker full of packaged meat. I'd only eaten elk once. To my palate, it far surpassed the venison I'd subsisted on the previous year. After one and often two meals of mule deer a day, the thought of another venison chop all but gagged me.

When I roused from my reflections on the deer that made an elk hunter out of me, I felt a little embarrassed. I'd just spent the second hour of my first-ever elk hunt dreaming of hunting rather than doing it. Still, the nap was rejuvenating. My head was now clear, my energy back. I was ready to resume my search for elk, with renewed determination.

I spent the rest of the morning slipping quietly through shadowy forest, soggy meadows, and brushy creek bottoms—always slinking in stealth mode. I avoided carelessly snapping small twigs or stumbling over random tangles of downed trees. Occasionally squatting to peer beneath low-hanging limbs, I paused to listen, to watch for any telltale movement, and then to listen some more. This was all about detecting the elk before the elk discovered me—the fine art of still hunting.

The undulating slope I'd been traversing for the past half hour was a likely place to find elk. I'd learned from scrutinizing such things the previous two summers for the U.S. Forest

Service that this blend of topography, forage plants, and cover was an elk's idea of good habitat. The game trails that webbed the forest floor were scattered with droppings. Then I faintly detected that smell—the one I instantly recognized as the sweet barnyard scent of elk having recently passed.

Pausing to listen, I glanced at my watch and was startled to find it was nearly 2:00 p.m. I crept another hundred yards or so to a small bump in the ridge guarded by a towering ponderosa pine. Its burn scars branded it a relic predating the last wildfire that had scorched this land.

My perch beneath the mother tree offered a good vantage point, and a good place to satisfy a ravenous hunger. I rifled through my pack, opened the first can of tuna, and drained the juice. Fingering the pale meat between two slices of bread, I wolfed the meal. Belatedly, I wondered if the pungent smell of the fish drifted far into the forest, raising a red flag to those unfamiliar with mountain albacore. A red squirrel seemed to answer my query with a staccato chorus of insults. As a token precaution, I heaped duff over the drained juice before downing the second can and the rest of my lunch.

I considered my position in relation to the truck, using a compass to orient a topo map spread across my lap. I made my best estimate by retracing my route across the contour lines. Old Blue was nearly two miles away. Pleased with my orienteering, I considered how best to use the rest of the day. I settled on 5:00 p.m., not 6:00, as the time that Ron and I had chosen to meet back at the truck. At least if I were wrong, I wouldn't keep him waiting.

Shortly, I realized the sporadic rustlings I attributed to red squirrels collecting and burying cones were something more. After two or three more minutes of strained listening, there it was—a distinct snap of a branch, followed by a sound like a bush gently shaken. I pinpointed the direction but saw nothing through the binoculars. Again, the rustle of vegetation and a muted snap. Energized and impatient, I carefully hoisted my rucksack and rifle. In a bent-kneed crouch, I crept across the slope, ever so slowly. Entering a denser patch of trees, I again heard rustling. *Now I must be close.* I peered through the sparse undergrowth of huckleberry and Labrador tea until a rusty-brown patch of movement caught my eye. Trying to control my breathing, I inched closer still and slipped the 8 mm Mauser to my shoulder and squinted through the scope. *Yes, definitely an elk!*

I could see much of the body but not the head or neck. I was sure the body color wasn't the subtly blonder coat of a bull. A calf would weigh half as much as a cow elk in late October. No, this was a big elk, not a calf.

I was now within forty yards. Plenty close. The elk turned in place, and my heart thumped. Did she smell me? The head and neck were now in plain view; and yes, it was a cow! I tucked the rifle into my shoulder, placed the scope's crosshairs at the base of her head, and . . .

The rifle's report exploded in my ears. Perhaps I flinched when I shot, because through the scope I now saw only tree trunks and brush. I waited a moment, listening. Only silence, beyond the pounding in my ears. So I raced ahead and found the elk lying limp on the ground.

It was almost surreal, the size of the animal, so much larger than the three deer that friends and I harvested the previous year on Rogers Pass. I was in awe of her muscled form and beautiful coat and, at the same time, dumbfounded by the reality that I had actually pulled this off. The impact was far out of proportion to life's events, I know, yet felt enormous at that moment.

I placed a palm on her warm shoulder and realized that I was touching something extraordinary. The rusty-brown sides were in sharp contrast to her chocolate head, belly, legs, and six-inch-long hair of her mane. The vestige of a tail—far smaller than on white-tailed or mule deer—blended perfectly into the burnt-orange rump patch, for which the Shawnee named the animal "wapiti." I brushed my hand from the silky mane back to her still flank. I thought about how much more amazing it would be to touch the living, breathing animal—something I couldn't conceive that I'd do hundreds of times in my future career.

I paused a few moments more, dwelling on fleeting images of the elk moving easily through the forest, constantly testing the air for danger with nostrils flared, rotating her ears toward faint sounds, stripping leaves from the huckleberry bushes that surrounded us. Tears trickled down my cheeks. My heart beat in my ears. These were such unexpected emotions. All I could do was thank the elk for the nourishment it would provide.

To me, the act of hunting is about the stalk and pursuit. The intensity is what makes hunting so different from seeking elk or other wildlife to observe or photograph. Hunting makes me think like the pursued, to see, hear, and smell as nearly as a deer or elk must do. It's about everything that happens along the way, whether I'm successful or not. It reminds me of a fly-fishing companion who, whenever asked, "How was the fishing?" responds, "The fishing's always great; the catching sometimes leaves something to be desired."

My focus turned to the task at hand. Before me lay five hundred pounds of flesh, bone, organs, and hide, measuring nearly eight feet from nose to rump. The meat, bundled tautly beneath the tightly stretched hide, would be sweet, lean, and unadulterated by the hormones, supplements, and antibiotics that course the veins of commercial livestock. Not until the elk was ferried home and carefully butchered in my backyard would my first elk hunt be complete.

After filling out the game tag attached to my hunting license, I began disemboweling the animal. Soon I was sweating and bathed in blood to my elbows. After rolling the entrails aside, some 30 percent of her mass, I paused to drink some water and realized I hadn't signaled Ron. I wiped my hands on a rag pulled from the rucksack and fired two quick shots, paused, and fired another.

Last year's deer we dragged easily from the forest. A foot of snow reduced friction and kept dirt and debris from soiling the body cavity. No such conditions today. An NFL linebacker couldn't drag this 350-pound carcass almost two miles to the truck. Just tugging the forequarters uphill to drain the pooled blood told me that.

I really hadn't considered how this next aspect of elk quest would unfold. Getting an elk this first day afield was unexpected. After all, only 20–30 percent of elk hunters are successful each year. I chose not to dwell on the details. When Ron joined me, we'd figure it out.

However we were to extract this elk from the woods, it wouldn't be in one piece. So after reloading the Mauser and signaling to Ron once more, I set to splitting the elk in two. First, I removed the head and lower legs by disarticulating joints. Then, I punctured the hide and worked the knife blade between the vertebrae where the T-bones become rib steaks. There, front and back halves.

Above me darkening billows sailed the sky like an armada of sixteenth-century galleons across the sea. I watched the sun settling beneath them toward the snowcapped Bitterroot peaks. In an hour or so, it would disappear.

I warmed to the crack of two quick shots followed by a third. They were close, so I shouted, "Hey, Ron! Over here!"

Ron and I exchanged highlights of the day's hunt. He had heard elk and gotten a fleeting glimpse of one. He grinned and slapped me on the back, demanding to know all about my success. Then we turned to the daunting task before us. After some head-scratching and discussion of elementary physics, we began by each dragging half the elk. It was mostly downhill to the truck, so gravity worked in our favor. However, our progress halted whenever we'd get tangled in brush or encountered a downed tree, which happened with great regularity. At such obstacles, we'd join forces to muscle each half, slung rifles beating us about the head and back. Despite the forty-degree temperature, sweat poured down our faces and soaked our clothes.

Besides our slow progress, I became discouraged that any flesh not protected by the elk's hide began resembling the forest floor. So, with nightfall looming and our canteens now empty, we resolutely hatched plan B. We'd string each half of the elk on a carry pole—you know, the way 1970s nature shows portrayed African Bushmen transporting impala back to camp. Finding two downed trees suitable for the job, we sawed them to length. We tied the front legs together and slid a pole between and then did the same with the hind half. *Voila!* Genius triumphs over adversity. Well, almost.

The plan was to hoist the pole and carry one half for a hundred yards or so, then leapfrog the other half a similar distance beyond the first. In practice, we found that the elk liked to swing beneath the pole and slide forward, trying to pass whoever was in front. But we were quick studies. After a near disaster when we both stumbled, we bound the legs to the centers of the poles.

The swinging, however, remained problematic and aggravated the biting of the pole into the tops of our shoulders. The hind half of the elk proved most hazardous. It hung lower and swayed more violently, a motion we tried desperately to prevent by walking in step and moving deliberately. Once the swinging started, however, it could only be halted when Ron or I yelled, "Stop!" or, "Oh shit!" to prevent the three of us from crashing to the ground.

This was distressing enough, but now twilight had ebbed into the black of night. The temperature plummeted in the face of a stiffening northwest wind, and wet snowflakes the size of quarters began plopping on us. We'd made scant headway down the mountain, and now our footing deteriorated on a glaze of icy snow.

Over the next three hours, we struggled. There were a couple of spectacular slips and falls along the way. I winced each time, as much for the elk as for myself. It struck me as disrespectful to treat the animal so, and I redoubled my efforts to be more careful each time.

Ultimately a dense stand of beargrass proved our undoing. This statuesque plant is not a grass at all, rather a robust flowering forb of montane forests and meadows of northwestern Montana. If you've never seen it in bloom, it's reminiscent of a limp-leaved yucca plant. From a basal whorl of shiny, evergreen leaves rises a central flowering stalk topped by a thickset bundle of cream-colored flowers that are relished by elk and other herbivores. Some stalks are tall enough to thump one in the head on a murky night. More perilous are the slippery leaves underfoot, especially when wet. Now varnished with snow, our patch of beargrass turned into toboggan city.

Through the pole, I felt Ron slip as he fumbled for our only flashlight. Its batteries were failing, so whoever was in the lead used it sparingly to check for dangers ahead or for our presumed position on the map. Without uttering so much as a strident "Dammit" both of his feet went out. He lurched down the slope, with the hindquarters attacking his backside. I joined them both in an unceremonious heap.

After the groaning ceased, my groping companion bellowed, "My glasses, my glasses . . . I lost my glasses!"

"Try the flashlight," I responded.

"Yeah, right. If I knew where it was, I would!" he protested.

We patted the snow around us. No missing specs. But I spotted the flashlight's faint beam behind Ron, and he retrieved it from beneath the snow. After several more minutes of looking and pawing, the glasses were nowhere to be found. Trying in vain to quell my amusement, I theorized they may have pitched into a tree. Ron offered a disdainful "Oh, bullshit" and an alternative theory that they lay crushed under the hindquarters of the elk. *That would be poetic justice*, I thought. We carefully rolled it over, the most gently it had been treated in the past couple of hours. But no squashed spectacles appeared.

We decried our pitiful situation for a few moments. Then Ron decisively exclaimed, "I'm not going any farther tonight."

He lamented that somebody was going to get killed . . . or at least a broken leg, or a gouged eye, or a hernia . . . or some other grievous injury. It flashed through my mind that Ron had become a pessimistic whiner, but it didn't seem the time to raise the topic. Besides, all those possibilities of bodily harm seemed imminent to me as well, once I stopped laughing. I agreed; we should abandon plan B.

We'd been leapfrogging the elk halves only a few dozen yards at a time. This saved using the flashlight excessively to locate the trailing half. Though uncertain of our position, we both felt we must be halfway back to Old Blue. Still, we'd exhausted our patience, food, and water, and long ago began eating snow. Ron outlined plan C: Build a fire beneath a sheltering Doug fir. Dry out. Maybe catch some shut-eye. Renew our efforts after daybreak. I halfheartedly offered an alternative: Just find our way back to the truck now. Retrieve the elk tomorrow. But as weariness engulfed me, I was no more enthused about continuing on than Ron.

We broke the innermost twigs and branches from the fir. Soon a fire crackled at our feet. As we slumped against the tree trunk, the aches began to set in . . . everywhere. It had been an ordeal. "Don't think we should do it this way next time," I deadpanned.

"Yeah, right," Ron sarcastically agreed. Before we could devise an inspired plan for retrieving next year's elk, we both nodded off.

In the fading glow of our little fire, we roused nearly an hour after midnight. Both of us were shivering. It had grown much colder. The snow had stopped, and brilliant stars now studded patches of moonlit sky among drifts of clouds. Illuminated clumps of beargrass, tree trunks, and branches shadowed a snowy backdrop, like a psychedelic mural. There was unqualified silence, as if we were the only souls left on the planet. We rose, stretched, groaned, and compared the severity of our respective aches. Simultaneously, we both blurted out, "Let's get out of here." And so we did, I leading Ron sans glasses.

Within an hour, we found our ride home. Another hour and I had dropped Ron off, pulled in front of my place, and tumbled into bed, where I slept like the dead. The next day, we returned to the scene of our escapade—Ron with his spare glasses, both of us with much-improved spirits.

The drive down Highway 93 is framed by the towering Bitterroot Range on the west and the darkly forested Sapphires on the east, places I widely traveled afoot and grew to love during my six years in Missoula. We recounted and laughed about the previous night's events. Ron showed off a badly bloodied elbow, a lump on his temple, a gash on his chin, and a bruised tailbone that I refused to look at. I complained of a black-and-blue hip and bum knee that were "certainly far worse" than his list of ailments. Both of us bemoaned our aching shoulders, but it was our bruised male egos that suffered most. Our misadventures led both of us to the same conclusion. Our first elk hunt was something we wouldn't soon forget.

We backtracked and retrieved the elk from where we had propped the two halves across a downed Douglas fir trunk. A pair of *wheeooing* Canada jays, perched near our dangling orange vests, welcomed us. But no scavengers had molested the meat. This time we skidded the halves over the snow on plastic tarps. Returning to Missoula well before dark, we congratulated ourselves on a hunt that had gone just as planned.

I've had many satisfying elk hunts since. Yet none do I remember as clearly as that one in 1973. That initial experience began a life of learning the joy of stalking elk. But I discovered much more. A fascination about the animal simmered inside of me. It helped channel my passion for wildlife and wildlands toward a thirty-year career as a wildlife scientist and manager. I still look forward to fall and pursuing wild elk. But with a boning knife and oversized pack, I now retrieve the elk in a kinder and gentler way.

SIX

WOODPECKERS TO GOATS

Climb the mountains and get their good tidings.

—John Muir, *The Mountains of California*

Walk into my home and one of the first things you will see is a mountain goat. The shoulder-mounted specimen I harvested in Montana's Bitterroot Mountains graces a ten-foot stone wall in the living room. When a guest learns that I studied mountain goats in that very mountain range, I'm often asked in astonishment, "How could you study those beautiful animals and then shoot one?" A logical reaction, I understand.

Actually, it happened in reverse. I drew a mountain goat permit in fall 1972, the first year I hunted big game. I had never conceived of hunting mountain goats; knew little about them; and in fact, had never seen one. But all of that changed the previous fall.

"Got plans for Thanksgiving?" asked Chuck, my college dorm mate at the University of Montana.

"No. Nothing special," I said.

"Want to come to Great Falls? My mom makes the best turkey dressing." My taste buds went on high alert. "We could hike around Sun River Game Range on the weekend," he continued. "There'll be some huge elk and mulies pushed down by the snow."

I'd moved from Michigan to Missoula in January 1971 to finish the last two years of an undergraduate degree in wildlife biology. My parents and sisters all lived back in Michigan, and I wasn't planning another marathon thirty-hour drive just a month before Christmas break.

"Sounds great. I'd love to," I replied. Considering my other option, hanging out at an abandoned campus, I was grateful.

At his parents' home, I learned that Chuck came from a long line of hunters. His bedroom walls were bedecked with trophies, all of which he'd taken by age eighteen. Heavily antlered white-tailed and mule deer heads, a stately pronghorn antelope, a full-curl bighorn, and a monster seven-point bull elk—the latter ruling a high-ceilinged living room wall. But the animal that drew my attention most was a billy, a male mountain goat.

"Where'd you get that?" My eyes fixed on the coal-black nose, curved ten-inch horns, and amber eyes contrasted against his flowing white coat and billy goat beard.

"Near the Chinese Wall in the Bob Marshall Wilderness," he beamed.

"Tell me the story," I invited. "That's the most handsome animal I've ever seen." As Chuck unwound his week in the wilderness—spotting far-off white dots on eroded tawny escarpments, and making heart-pounding ascents to sneak within range—the seed of my curiosity about mountain goats was sown.

On the drive back to Missoula, we covered the usual topics—classes, fishing, and girls. "What about those goats?" I steered the conversation. "Are there any near Missoula? Someplace close to see them?"

"Sure. Just south of town, in the Selway-Bitterroot Wilderness Area," he said. "I think it's the biggest population in the state."

On a frigid December day, I spotted my first mountain goats in Bass Creek canyon. Several clung to gray granite walls, hundreds of feet above the streamside trail. I coerced friends to join me on other weekend excursions into the Bitterroots' glacier-gouged chasms. With each sighting, I became more beguiled by this "beast the color of winter," as biologist Douglas Chadwick titled the first book written about the species. But the hunter in me pushed me further.

Along with others questing a challenge, I applied through Montana's lottery drawing for one of the seventy-five hunting permits available for the Bitterroots' goats. Miraculously, I was one of the successful applicants among a few hundred who had applied. From the last week of October through November 1972, I spent thirteen awesome days chasing what seemed to be ghosts. (I know, there aren't thirteen Saturdays and Sundays in five weeks. Okay, I cut a few classes that fall.)

By the hunting season's final week, I had exhausted hunting partners.

"No thanks," said Ron. "I've got a silviculture test to study for."

"You're nuts," another responded to my offer for a leisurely day away from classes. "If I wanted a heart attack, I'd run a marathon or, better yet, go on a donut binge!" Ben reminded me of our earlier three-day trip in search of goats. "Like a military forced march" is how he described the pace.

"It's supposed to dump up high," my friend Pete replied. "You'll be butt-deep in snow."

Of course, he was right. But like the biggest billies, I was undeterred by such trifles. Bucking snow and cheating steep chutes of avalanche victims was part of the challenge. Call me crazy. I respected the hazards, but I didn't fear them. I just wanted to be up there. Sharing the goats' domain—if only temporarily—made me feel fully alive, literally on top of the world.

So, on a radiant day tagging after a major winter storm, I trudged upward into Montana's Big Sky, alone, with my spirits soaring. I hiked a ridge rising between two parallel canyons. These U-shaped twin gorges were bulldozed by Pleistocene glaciers and carved relentlessly still deeper into the earth's crust by grinding streams. Breathtaking country! My destination, unless

I encountered a suitable (meaning a large male) mountain goat sooner, was a 9,300-foot summit 2,500 feet above where I'd left my car at daybreak. St. Mary Peak was one of the highest in the Bitterroot Range, the kind of remote and desolate place where a goat may survive to old age. I hadn't hunted or even hiked here before, but an old native of the Bitterroot Valley who'd spent years hunting elk in the Selway-Bitterroot Wilderness told me he'd often seen goats to the west of St. Mary. This was the promise that drove my legs through a knee-deep blanket of snow.

To the goat hunter, the only value of snow is that a dump in the high country will drive his quarry down off the peaks. But the fall's accumulation had been insufficient to force the goats toward their winter ranges. It only made trudging at elevation more painstaking and the goats more difficult to spot on a canvas of white.

After three miles, I left the trail where it switchbacked to St. Mary's summit. A mile farther west and one thousand feet of elevation higher loomed a rocky promontory that I aimed to crest on the south running shoulder of St. Mary. As I left the last scattered trees behind, an expanse of stunted whitebark pines and subalpine firs blocked my route to the far ridge's rise. At 8,500 feet of elevation, blistering winds had warped the trees into a tangled thicket no more than five feet high. This zone of krummholz (from the German, meaning "crooked wood") is the altitudinal limit of subalpine forest, which grows higher on mountainsides near the equator, progressively lower toward the earth's poles. If krummholz is good at anything, it's good at collecting windblown snow. I found myself wallowing waist-deep in snow packed into the clutching snarl of twisted trunks.

After nearly an hour, I emerged from that maze. The talus field in front of me rose abruptly to the sky. Except for scattered drifts, winds had swept the barren slope mostly free of snow. What vegetation existed hunkered in crevices between the rocks.

With renewed spirits, I scrambled toward the top. In the thin, chill air, I halted every few minutes to catch my breath and gaze above me for any sign of life. Nothing moved except the steam that billowed from my mouth. Amid the stark sterility of snow and rock, it seemed not even a mountain goat could make a living here.

I trudged upward. As the grade steepened, I slung the German Mauser rifle overhead onto my back so that both hands were free to catch my balance when a gust of wind or an ill-placed step made me teeter. Then suddenly—whether I saw it or merely sensed it—I detected movement above. The unexpected sight of the shaggy body caught me wholly by surprise. The image made my oxygen-starved heart pound even faster. I crouched and scooted behind a nearby boulder. Resting the rifle across the top, I peered through the scope and located what was a big billy goat. Just then, he stopped walking and swung his head over his shoulder. Coal-black eyes riveted on me—his undoing as it turned out.

During a struggle of conflicted emotions, I tried to persuade my index finger to squeeze the trigger.

Here's your chance.

But how can I kill such a beautiful animal?

This is why you've spent thirteen days on wind-blasted ridges, freezing your ass.

But he belongs up here, not reduced to steaks and a mounted showpiece.

He's headed over the ridge. It's now or never.

It was the most tortured I've ever felt about taking an animal's life.

The field dressing, caping, skinning, and butchering with half-numb hands consumed nearly two hours, far more time than I'd imagined. My tingling cheeks and nose relayed that the temperature was falling—probably into the teens and much colder with the windchill. Finally, with my canvas rucksack bulging with meat, and the animal's head and hide lashed to the outside with parachute cord, I started down the mountain in the waning alpenglow.

The descent soon turned harrowing. Clouds rolled across the snowbound ridges to the west. The afternoon wind had buried my furrowed trail through the snow. At last light, I targeted a distant, skeletal whitebark pine. A more southerly route to that stubborn guardian at the forest margin would circumvent the krummholz belt—a quagmire in daylight, a certain nightmare to negotiate in the dark. Under the pack straps' burning weight, I forged ahead, down the mountain.

After darkness engulfed me, I must have veered off course. *Something's not right. The ground's giving way too fast.*

I unshouldered my pack and rifle and shuffled a few steps more. My feet slid and bumped tentatively to a stop. Beneath a moonless sky, I squinted, trying to penetrate the veil that enveloped me. For the first time, I questioned what I was doing here—alone, in the dark, still some two thousand feet above my parked car. I flicked on my pocket flashlight and aimed its pale beam a few feet beyond me. The mountain's dusky, frozen mantle vanished into black space.

An eerie foreboding crept over me, as if I were walking blindfolded in an unknown place. Then I recognized the soft chorus of Big Creek, murmuring four thousand feet below.

"Oh my God!" I gasped. I'd almost walked off the canyon wall. I took a few deep breaths, willing my heart to slow and clear thinking to prevail.

As the panic subsided, I remembered the compass tucked in a side pocket of my pack. Unzipping the pocket and plucking it from inside, a wave of relief, almost joy, swept over me. This simple device and a topographic map were the best friends that a mountaineer could have in the days before GPS units revolutionized orienteering. The map was now of limited use, given that I'd lost track of my location. But the compass would serve as my guide to intercept the forest trail, if only the dim light of my flashlight lasted. *Now why didn't I check the flashlight's brightness this morning? Put a spare set of batteries in my pack?* Note to self for future adventures.

I redirected my course to the northeast, angling away from the void of Big Creek canyon. Twenty more minutes of mindless slogging led me to the upper reaches of forest that cloaked the lower mountain. The trees tempered the wind, and soon I found my tracks from that morning punched in the snow. Three hours later, I burst through the door of my apartment.

"Hey, everybody, wake up!" I whooped. Ben, Chuck, and Ron, my college roommates, rolled out of bed and joined me in the kitchen, where the prize strapped to my pack lay on the floor. As I regaled them with the story, someone broke out a six-pack to toast my success. Amid the celebration, I realized I was beat, mentally and physically exhausted from the day's exertion. But mostly I was thankful—thankful that I was still alive.

🌲

The course of a person's life can change so suddenly. The previous summer, I'd worked for the Lolo National Forest's staff wildlife biologist. One of my assignments was to record habitat preferences across the Lolo of North America's largest woodpecker, the pileated (the slightly larger ivory-billed woodpecker of the southeastern United States was already considered extinct). Measuring up to nineteen inches long with a thirty-inch wingspan, this crow-sized bird sports a conspicuous red crest that contrasts with its black-and-white body.

The work included mapping my observations of this distinctive woodworker and its handiwork. With their powerful bills, they excavate fist-sized, rectangular holes in dead and dying trees in search of carpenter ants and wood-boring beetle larvae— critters that foresters consider pests. They also nest in cavities that they excavate—very large cavities requiring very large trees.

Thus, the pileated is an obligate resident of old-growth forests of both coniferous and deciduous varieties.

Some ecologists consider the pileated a keystone species, because its feeding and nest excavations provide habitat for many other species. Once abandoned, these holes provide homes for forest songbirds, owls, squirrels, and even tree-nesting ducks. The pileated is the building contractor. Other species become tenants after the woodpecker moves on.

Catching a glimpse of this flying jackhammer, hearing its jungle bird call, and recording what trees in which areas bore its stamp of approval fascinated me. So taken was I by this red-crested carpenter that I hoped to conduct graduate research on its role in forest health.

But my experiences during the fall of 1972 in the mountain goat's domain prompted an abrupt change of plans. Hungry to learn more about goats, I read all that I could find and queried professors. As a senior thesis toward my undergraduate degree, I undertook a census of goats in several Bitterroot canyons during the winter of 1973. Each weekend from January through March, I traipsed four to five miles up each canyon, scanning the cliffs hundreds of feet above in search of wooly, white specks. Armed with binoculars and a sixty-power spotting scope, I was determined to find every last individual in their mountain kingdom.

Throughout those months, I learned that hunting seasons were based as much on professional intuition as on the scant field data informing wildlife managers about the population's status and well-being. No one of authority disputed that. In fact, the Montana Fish and Game Department had identified learning about the Bitterroot goats as the second-highest research priority in the state. Two years earlier, a student began the study but found the Bitterroot terrain too challenging. How fortunate for me. The population ecology of the goats became the subject of my master's degree research.

To describe the goat population—its size and composition, reproduction and survival, food habits and seasonal movements—I focused my efforts on six wilderness canyons. Glaciers had carved each ten to twelve miles eastward from the crest of the Bitterroots' spine toward the Bitterroot River valley below. When snow smothered the high country, a discrete herd of one to three dozen animals remained bound to south-facing walls of each Bitterroot canyon. With their favorable sun angle and snow-shedding, forty-degree-angled ramparts, these were the precarious asylums of goats until snowmelt freed the cliff dwellers in May.

In the mountain goat's domain, winters last half the year. The smothering snow and sunless canyon bottoms can feel cheerless, even claustrophobic. Yet the three winters I studied mountain goats were transcendent times. Traveling by snowshoe and cross-country skis and camping four miles beyond the nearest plowed road, I became enthralled by these "old men of the mountains" and by the remote, rugged wilds where they lived. It was a voiceless kingdom in which the whooshing of snowshoes, the wind in the pines, or the call of a gray jay were all that interrupted the rhythm of my own breathing most days. The mountain goat's sanctuary became my home and research lab.

After eighteen months in the Bitterroots, with my teaching assistantship ended, my GI Bill allocation expired, and a small research grant about to run out, I felt I had just scratched the surface. There remained so much yet to learn about these gravity-defying cliff dwellers and how they survived six-month winters in a vertical world. A third year of study seemed essential. I lobbied my graduate committee to grant me more time in the Bitterroots to gather more data. On a scant research stipend, I spent another year, through June 1975, in the mountain monarchs' stronghold.

To understand the goats' habits and wanderings beyond their snowbound winter subsistence, I spent June to mid-October 1974 backpacking through 150 square miles of wilderness. As I rambled the high ridges and cirques with sixty pounds of gear strapped on my back, balance, agility, and mountaineering know-how became as natural as the act of breathing. I fancied the self-reliance that remote country demanded without so much as a walkie-talkie for support (cell phones were not yet thought of). Where generations of sure-footed goats fattened and raised their kids, my bones might go undiscovered for decades. Yet this was surely as alive as I had ever been.

Month by month the goats' way of life grew clearer. Their ranges expanded in size, into the alpine in summer until the first snowstorms sent them retreating from the highest peaks to the lower canyons in autumn.

Some Bitterroot canyons had good road access to trailheads, even a mile or so up their lower reaches. In others, like Big Creek, logging roads up the intervening ridges between canyons provided motorized access above goat cliffs. This rendered goat herds more vulnerable to hunters than in canyons without such access. As a consequence, I learned that a disproportionate amount of each fall's harvest came from the more accessible drainages.

To sustain each canyon's goat herd, I proposed a remedy. Subdivide the Bitterroots into smaller hunting units to account for these access disparities. As numbers dwindled in future years, the idea belatedly took hold. This and my opposition to the logging of ridges above the goats' winter cliffs were my first forays into the politics of resource management. I'd get lots more practice during my career.

♣

During an interview about *Life on the Rocks*, my 2014 book about mountain goats, a journalist asked me this question: "Weren't you afraid, following those goats on the cliffs during winter and miles from other people?"

The inquiry made me pause, trying to recapture my mindset and sense of security some four decades in the past. Indeed, I sometimes found myself in situations that would petrify most flatlanders or turn back anyone unaccustomed to spending day after day far from civilization. On more than one occasion, the footing on icy ledges turned treacherous, or night closed in as I picked my way across boulder fields and escarpments on my return to camp. Other times, gravity unleashed the snowpack that crashed down canyon walls while I was stalking animals to capture and radio-collar or measuring their feeding habits high on the cliffs. Wilderness living stacks the odds against survival of the timid and unfit.

As I considered the reporter's question, my answer came from a familiar place—a place that predated my time in the Bitterroot Mountains. I can trace the spark back to childhood when my parents bought their first home, a modest two-story craftsman poised on a small hill above Muskegon Lake. There I spent countless days exploring the cattail marshes, mapping muskrat houses, and spying on red-winged blackbird nests. Although small in scale, it was a rich habitat where turtles paddled, frogs croaked, and crickets buzzed throughout summer nights.

My nerve was tested and honed during the year I spent as a combat marine. If I could survive all that my machine gun squad and I endured in the jungles and rice paddies of Vietnam, I could handle most anything. "Failure is not an option" became my motto.

So to the reporter I replied that I was never really afraid, despite winter's weather and rugged terrain. I paid attention to detail. I learned to respect the mountains and my provisional place within them. As my climbing skills and bushcraft matured, so did my passion to be among the goats, wherever they climbed. The joy I realized from the challenges and physical work of finding and studying those remarkable beasts made each day a new adventure. Each day prompted new questions about the lives of the animals but also new insights into their conservation needs.

And when the enveloping silence and isolation triggered twinges of loneliness, a nanny's doting care of her puffball offspring or the ethereal call of a pileated woodpecker echoing through a canyon reminded me of my good fortune. I had the rest of my life to live among the bustle of civilization, but only this short time to be immersed in truly wild nature.

SEVEN

THE BEAR AND THE TREE

Everything is funny, as long as it's happening to somebody else.
—Will Rogers, *The Illiterate Digest*

I cut my teeth on backcountry work with wildlife during the last two years of my undergraduate education at the University of Montana. Those summer jobs provided my first working taste of field biology, particularly studying elk, an iconic western species that sportsmen and conservationists hold dear and the animal that would later become a focus of my career.

Across the American West, elk inhabit remote, forested areas much of the year. But during the 1960s and continuing into the 1970s, it's fair to say that many western forests were under siege. The dizzying pace of timber cutting and road building degraded natural habitats and accelerated human impacts on wildlife across western public lands. It's true that logging of forests opened new feeding areas for deer and elk. As grass-es and shrubs sprouted and flourished following logging, the wildlife should follow . . . or so the theory went. However, that represented just one side of the equation. Elk and deer also need security cover—habitat in which to hide and feel safe.

The earliest studies indicated that elk abandoned areas of ac-tive logging, displaced up to one mile away. After the trees were cut and hauled to the mills, elk continued to avoid habitat within one-tenth mile and sometimes up to one mile—depending on topography—from newly constructed logging roads. Motorized access to formerly remote areas also increased hunter success, at least until most surviving elk had left. My summer work during 1972 and 1973 for western Montana's Lolo National Forest was focused on that issue.

Across the Lolo, a sprawling patchwork of clear-cut acreage evidenced the Forest Service's resource priorities at that time. Thousands more acres on the Lolo were planned for cutting in roadless tracts of big trees coveted by the forest's ambitious timber-management staff. By comparison with the forestry program's ample budget and staff, Gary Halvorson, a sandy-haired, lean, soft-spoken man of forty, was the Lolo Forest's only wildlife biologist. More than once I watched him return still seething and dispirited from a meeting where more pristine forest was proposed for saw logs. It wasn't just that Gary was forever playing defense, pressed to justify why habitat for these or those species in this or that watershed shouldn't be clear-cut. Ostensibly, the outcome was often a foregone conclusion, as he faced ten to twenty foresters hell-bent on "getting the cut out."

It worked like this: Regional Foresters handed down annual timber harvest targets to national forests, like generals issuing orders to marines. Targets were measured in "millions of board feet." Meeting those targets figured into performance evaluations of staff and supervisors . . . and perhaps promotion potential. Gary seemed to me a lone voice in the wilderness. He was the gloomy Gus reacting to the current crisis. He alone spoke for the wildlife that had no voice. These were the days before environmental impact statements and legal challenges to timber cuts were in vogue. As a lowly field technician Gary had hired, I was in no position to help. Still, I felt deeply sympathetic.

In 1973 Gary went on the offensive. To better defend wildlife needs—and to keep one step ahead of the chainsaws and dozers—he initiated an inventory of elk ranges in five planning units of the Lolo. That's where my fellow biological technician, Tad, and I came in. Our job was to canvass these roadless tracts of de facto wilderness, each greening tens of thousands of acres, and to record evidence of elk on the landscape.

Dropped by helicopter on another far-flung ridge each Monday morning, we spent the week tromping a new tract of Montana backcountry. Then, on Friday, we hiked to a prearranged point where our ride home had been left for us.

At each week's workplace, our job was to hike the length of every stream course above five thousand feet of elevation, including creases in mountainsides that only trickled snowmelt in spring. Compass, altimeter, and topographic maps in hand, we plotted watering holes, mineral licks, rutting wallows, trail systems, and localized concentrations of elk feeding and bedding sites.

Mineral licks are pockets of soils rich in salts relished by elk. Rutting wallows are commonly found where bulls gather harems during breeding season, clearly a biologically important time of the year for elk. Wallows are to elk what beer joints are to some college guys, a stop on the way to finding romance. In these muddy depressions, bull elk in rut roll and urinate on themselves in anticipation of mating. College guys . . . well, let's just say the analogy is correct in concept, but not in specifics.

For sixteen weeks, we camped beneath the stars, wolfed heaps of freeze-dried food, enjoyed breathtaking landscapes, saw loads of wildlife, almost never saw people, and lost what little baby fat either of us had. It was a blast!

In some respects, it was a treasure hunt, always into a new corner of the forest we'd never seen. Along the way, we found old trapper cabins—the roofs often collapsed and the interiors littered with old cans, rusted tools, and telltale newsprint. The hand-hewn logs spoke of a time when men were men and beaver grew scarce. On occasion, a rocky fire ring overgrown by vegetation, a sun-bleached elk skull with antlers hacked off, or a well-worn horseshoe showed the passage of unknown souls. At other times, I felt sure no other human had ever set foot where my boots trod. Such places included mucky alder thickets, ancient fir forests choked with deadfall, and slick slopes "steeper than a cow's face," in mountain-folk speak.

To cover more ground, Tad and I split up each morning. We moved in stealth mode like a hunter on a hot trail to increase our chances of stealing upon elk and spying on their daily lives.

Bushwhacking miles each day, from one small drainage to the next, I'd creep to thin ridgetops, never knowing to what I'd be treated on the other side. A group of elk calves prancing across a meadow under the watchful eyes of their mothers. A bull thrashing a spindly fir to strip the remaining velvet from hardening antlers.

Sounds and smells were telltale signals of nearby elk. A sharp bark from a cow to warn herdmates of scented danger. The languid talk of cows and calves winding through lime on parchment aspen groves. The mewing of calves floating softly across a basin on the breeze. And by late August, the bugling of bulls in rut erupting in earnest. Not just the occasional warm-up I strained to locate earlier in summer. No, these were strident shrieks, bellows, and grunts that announced their readiness for love and war.

♣

Over the summer, Tad and I often encountered elusive predators, a luxury of wilderness travel where humans and their trails were scarce. We spotted all the endemic carnivores: coyote, red fox, bobcat, weasel, mink, and pine marten. Only the reclusive mountain lion escaped our eyes, though some surely saw us. Because we were always in prime habitat for black bears and sometimes grizzlies, we carried a two-way radio. This was our lone safety net. We checked in with the Lolo Forest's dispatcher each morning at eight. Two missed calls and a search party would be organized to find and retrieve our remains.

Encounters with bears—like clouds of mosquitoes, rain-slicked beargrass, and wet socks—come with the work of many field biologists in western wildlands. During that summer of 1973, Tad and I had more run-ins with bears than most people have in a lifetime. Even on days that we didn't see bears, we saw their spoor—tracks in mud and piles of dung riddled with pinecone scales, deflated berries, ant exoskeletons, occasionally hair, and all manner of soft vegetation.

Bears have favorite foods but, unlike people, no corner grocery store. Their 24/7 food mart is whatever is in season and can be grazed or caught. Besides gathering grass and nuts, bulbs and berries, insects and larvae, they hunt fish and various rodents. Some are proficient at stalking and killing young deer, elk, moose, and caribou, something I would study twenty years later in my career. Bears are also content to eat carrion as an opportunistic protein source, just as our early ancestors sometimes did.

The four months that Tad and I gobbled gorp and freeze-dried meals are testament that humans, like bears, will eat most anything. We often perked up these desiccated facsimiles with fresh food we foraged: wild berries and salads of glacier lily blossoms and mushrooms. With our simple digestive systems, compared to the complex stomachs of ruminants like elk, and our teeth evolved over millennia for grinding fibrous plant foods as well as meat, our food-processing equipment share many generalist adaptations with the omnivorous bears. Our species' common anatomy, food habits, and other behaviors forged a special kinship between Native Americans and bears.

Besides their feces, other clues left in the forest indicated the presence of bears. Tufts of hair snagged on the bark of firs and pines registered where bears with an itch had rubbed. More unsettling, the beasts also marked the trunks of trees by clawing and biting them. The largest bears gouged scratches six feet and more above the ground.

So why do bears mark trees? Most hypotheses suggest important social functions. Males might be announcing dominance during the summer mating season; perhaps females are reinforcing territorial boundaries as a means to avoid other females; or bears may scar trees for orientation when they enter unknown areas. Another unsolved mystery of nature, it seems.

By summer's end we learned that these markings weren't entirely random. Rather, some seemed like road signs displayed along well-used travel routes. Whatever their purpose, the vertical gouges and stripped bark forewarned us like neon traffic signs. *Be alert. Bear was here!*

All of this was known to countless other outdoorsmen. But these lessons in natural history were nascent discoveries to us.

♣

Within the Lolo National Forest, black bears prowled every hideaway that Tad and I tramped to map the presence of elk and record their habits. But in two of the more remote areas we worked, bumping into a grizzly bear was also a possibility.

My first experience with the black bear's larger relative, *Ursus horribilis*, was a didactic rather than menacing encounter. Tad and I were mapping elk habitat on the flank of Big Hole Peak, a skyward bulge in a block of Montana mountains. A mile from camp one morning, we came across a meadow furrowed as if a mini earthmover had been at work. In mounds of freshly excavated soil, we found five-inch-wide paw marks. On the wider front paw, claw tips clearly registered two to three inches beyond the pad. These were not a black bear's wimpy one-inch claws. No, this was *grizzly*! With their oversized claws, grizzlies unearth tender bulbs of spring beauties and biscuitroot. This bear, however, was past the salad course; he was digging for an entrée of three-ounce pocket gophers.

These small rodents tunnel networks of shallow subways, likewise in search of starchy tubers and roots. Raised ridges of soil, like a rodent road map, trace their passage across a meadow's surface. In underground larders, the gophers stash harvested food that's crammed and transported in cheek pouches. These stores provide a wholesome delight for the omnivorous grizzly, too, when the more elusive rodents scurry away.

On a distant bald ridge, we spied a lone bear ambling toward the forest. The distinctive shoulder hump and shimmer of silver-tipped fur confirmed the first sighting of a grizzly for either of us outside Yellowstone and Glacier National Parks. Pure wonderment prickled my nerves at this near-mythical sight. This was the animal that struck awe and fear in the hearts of Lewis and Clark's expedition members, for it recognized no superior.

This giant's dwindling population was federally recognized as threatened with extinction in 1973. I could only marvel at the grizzly's perseverance under intense human persecution and commandeering of its domain. Standing on its saucer-sized tracks I felt certain that the bear belonged to this place as much as the spring beauties, gophers, and the mountain itself.

Compared to this benign encounter with the grizzly, Tad and I each had nerve-racking experiences with the animal's less fearsome cousin, the black bear. Mine was in a jungle of fir and spruce in the Sapphire Mountain Range, south of Missoula. This old-growth forest was strewn with downed trees, often so densely jackstrawed that treading their trunks offered the only practical way to get around. Footing was always uncertain. When wet, the jacket of moss and lichen proved slippery. Worse yet was the tendency of bark to peel unpredictably from logs underfoot. Patience and balance were indispensable assets for navigating these aerial causeways.

I began crossing a fallen spruce, nearly three feet in diameter. It spanned a steep-sided drainage incising the mountain. Arms outstretched like a tightrope walker and riveted on each step's placement, I inched along, centering one step after the other, pressing through spiny-needled branches that poked from the trunk.

Halfway across the spruce and some eight feet above a tangle of smaller debris, I sensed something. Not a sound. Not a smell. Just a presence. Raising my eyes from the scaly gray bark, a bear stared back with penetrating, dark eyes. Poised half erect, its front feet were on the far end of the same log where I now teetered. Worse yet, she had two cubs in tow.

I'd been told that encounters with bears with small cubs were encounters of the worse kind. Given a chance, a black bear invariably will flee from a human—at least in places like this, where they are hunted. But protective mothers may respond defensively at close quarters. A sow's greatest dread is confronting a boar black bear or grizzly that may kill her cubs. A human, even a well-intentioned biologist, might be considered a similar threat. In short order, mother bears must choose to flee or stay and fight.

My instincts said, *Be the baddest boar in the woods.* With no time to think this through, I went on the offensive. In my scariest bear imitation, I raised my arms and hoarsely barked several times at her as loud as I could, "Wuff."

She hesitated, glanced back at her cubs, and returned a menacing stare at me. *Okay, this is it,* I thought. *Reduced to the bottom of the food chain.*

To my immense relief, she turned and bolted into the forest, wuffing to her cubs, who scurried up nearby trees. With my heart thumping like a sprinter's, I eased my butt down and straddled the log to regain my composure. I now understood the mountain climber's expression about "sewing machine legs."

♦

My run-in with the black bear and two cubs who played that game of chicken with me paled in comparison to Tad's most unnerving experience. Returning to camp late one evening, he related his ordeal. He'd been slinking along a ribbon of alders that crowded a trickle of water. Flanking the rivulet was a meadow on one side and scattered firs on the other. As midday approached, he chose a sturdy Douglas fir near the alders to rest his back and lunch beneath.

Tad was a pretty fair photographer and carried his Nikon and several lenses everywhere. After mounting the camera atop an aluminum tripod, he trained the telephoto on a gap in the tangle of alders and then broke out a tuna sandwich. It was one of those summer days when one relishes being alive in the backcountry. The only sounds are nature's; and one could imagine, if only for the day, that none of the trappings of civilization lay just a few miles distant. A face full of sun and the mountains' serenity are all one needs.

Then, movement upstream. The twelve-foot tops of alders shuddered. *Listen.* A twig snapped.

Tad stiffened, and leaned forward. He checked the camera's focus on the breach in the alder thicket. Anticipation rose in his chest. *A bull elk, antlers dressed in velvet? A moose winding its way toward a midday snack of willows?* He couldn't tell.

The animal advanced, but without the distinctive cadence of hooves that had become so familiar over the past two months. Just the sporadic brush of shrubs on body. And then, framed by alders, materialized the largest bear Tad had seen all summer. The snout of the massive black head tilted up, sniffing the air for signals. Deliberately, the muzzle turned as the eyes trained squarely on Tad.

"I had no idea how fast I could climb a sap-smeared fir," Tad said, the seriousness of the situation etched in his face.

Battering branches aside with head and shoulders, he plowed from limb to limb. "Still, the bear charged so quickly that when I glanced down, he was leaning upright against the trunk."

Its jaws were agape just beyond Tad's size nines. *Climb! Climb! Climb!* He told himself.

"I climbed until I got wedged in a whorl of branches, twenty feet up the tree," he lamented.

"But it was a black bear, right?" I tried to confirm. "If you stood your ground, it probably would've bluff charged. Besides, black bears climb trees."

"I know, but this was no ordinary bear. He meant business," Tad replied without a hint of defensiveness. "I just went for the tree out of self-preservation."

In the same situation, maybe I'd have done the same, I thought. The tenet "face a black bear, climb from a grizzly" has its foundation. Black bears climb; grizzlies rarely do. And a black bear attack, not a bluff charge, should be met aggressively. He probably sees you as prey. Fight for your life. Whereas grizzlies more often charge out of defense of food or young, an arboreal escape avoids testing their appetites. But fear can overrule such logic.

Now, temporarily wedged between branches, Tad feared his reaction to climb, rather than face the bear, might end poorly. There was no assurance that this aggressive bruin wouldn't follow him. Maybe climbing just postponed a mauling.

Initially the bear made a variety of unnerving bellows and grunts, followed by whacking the tree with a front paw. He then turned his ire on alternate victims. He cuffed the camera and tripod to the ground and plundered Tad's daypack. The remains of lunch devoured, he returned to torment Tad for another forty minutes. His behavior varied from circling the tree and assaulting Tad with vocal insults to more thoughtfully musing (as Tad imagined it) about how long a human might remain up a tree.

Tad expected the worst. "So I broke off a limb to use as a jab stick, just in case the bear decided to come up. I'm lucky—I guess he was too fat to try."

Tad was rather reserved by nature, so his flailing hands and agitated reenactment quite convinced me of the seriousness of the ordeal. But he kept using the pronoun "he," so I just had to ask him during a pause in the action, "How did you know the bear was a male?"

"Christ's sake!" he howled, "He looked as big as my Volkswagen!" Besides, he reasoned, the beast was far too aggressive for a female without cubs, and this was mating season.

Good enough logic for me. "Yeah," I concurred. "He must've been all hopped up on testosterone."

The bear made one last flurry. Upright against the tree, he thrust his bulk sufficiently against the trunk that Tad felt the tremor and readied the jab stick for action. "If I had to, I was gonna poke him in the eye or maybe the nose," he insisted. Then grinning, he conceded, "Like that would've done any good. Probably woulda given him a better reason to eat me."

Finally, the bear just walked into the forest, in search of his love interest or maybe a banquet of carpenter ants and groundsels.

At the tale's conclusion, I congratulated Tad on his clear thinking and being able to remain calm under pressure. "I'm glad you're okay. Everything turned out alright, so you did the right thing."

Those were somewhat self-serving comments, since I was the team leader and responsible for the safe conduct of our work. I surely didn't want a performance review marred by the unfortunate demise of a coworker. That's when Tad confessed the unthinkable. He became so anxious at one point in the tree that he thought he'd pee his pants. Besides emptying his aching bladder, he hoped this indignity would dishearten his tormentor. So carefully directing the course of the stream, he let go from aloft. The bear was unfazed by the shower.

EIGHT

GRAVITY

> Apparently there is nothing that cannot happen today.
> —Mark Twain, *Autobiography of Mark Twain*

It's a universal truth of mountaineering: gravity happens; and it happens fast. The more tilted the terrain and terrifying the exposure, the graver are gravity's penalties for mistakes. Yet a gutsy community of critters calls such places home. And among North America's large mammal species, none braves the odds more than the mountain goat.

Nearly four decades after my field studies in the Selway-Bitterroot Wilderness Area, those shaggy cliff dwellers still crowd my Likes page. Even after spending so much time among them in Montana, Idaho, and Washington, I still look forward to my next excursion into goat range. Whether clinging stoically to snow-draped cliffs or grazing flowered, alpine meadows, their very existence strikes me as remarkable.

Others are enamored by eagles or elephants, parrots or pandas, maybe even meerkats or turtles. As much as anything, the animals that tug our heartstrings reveal our human individuality. Mammals garner the lion's share of attention. With their adorable eyes, familiar shapes, and pleasantly furry bodies, that's understandable. In other mammals, we most closely see ourselves; and humans, it seems, are most enamored with ourselves.

In plain language, I'm a big fan of the mountain goat and its lofty lifestyle. Persevering in precipitous places 365 days each year is dangerous business for sure. Outwardly, goats effortlessly rule their vertical world with equal measures of climbing aptitude and patience. But perils lie everywhere. Most are the products of gravitational pull.

Throughout its western range, observers recount that even this ace of alpinists is subject to missteps and tumbles. I once watched in horror as a nanny and kid, while attempting to turn around, both fell fifteen feet from a dead-end sliver of ledge. The kid landed upright, unharmed. The nanny was not so fortunate. She crashed back first onto a juniper bush, inflicting a nasty wound on her foreleg. This is a cost of life on steep rocks, where security and danger are oddly intertwined.

As an indicator of injury suffered from climbing accidents, I measured horn breakage in a sample of 123 Bitterroot goats harvested by hunters. On 30 percent, one or both horns were broken. Many older animals had loose, chipped, or missing front teeth, possibly the products of falls. Biologist Douglas Chadwick's painstaking observations of mountain goats in northwestern Montana confirmed that goats younger than two suffered 80 percent of all climbing accidents. There's no substitute for experience in mountaineering.

Besides a goat's own unforced errors while navigating cliffs, there are those hazards that mountain climbers term "objective dangers," such as falling rocks and sliding snow. While rockfall may occasionally strike an ill-placed goat, avalanches are a far greater danger on many goat ranges. During the day, exposed rock absorbs solar energy and melts adjacent snow, which flows and later freezes under large snowfields. Fluctuation of temperatures around the freezing point causes slabs of snow, both small and immense, to slide off ledges, crash over crags, and plunge down debris chutes, carrying ice, rock, and trees along for the ride. This is not a good time to live on a cliff. And goats seem well aware of that. When an avalanche rumbles down the mountain, goats scramble against rock walls or duck beneath overhangs. Their panic is palpable.

From March through early May is when many a goat is swept away. Their crumpled bodies, deposited in avalanche run outs, serve as carrion for bears, coyotes, eagles, and ravens. Thus, the Old Man of the Mountains pays a price for his precarious security in an environment where predators and competitors are few but where the elements take a toll.

I can attest to these hazards in the tilted terrain that our mountain goats call home. While navigating the high country, I once became caught in an avalanche—one that I inadvertently triggered.

It was late November, not an avalanche-prone time of year. In most mountain ranges, after tons of snow have accumulated in layers, late winter and spring are the seasons of white thunder. The snowbound slope I intended to traverse, at eight thousand feet of elevation, showed no signs of previous slides. Turns out, that was merely a matter of timing. Gravity lacked only the incentive to do its thing.

I began crossing, kicking steps in the snowy mantle to provide a firm platform for footing. This was the dawn of my mountaineering days, long before taking a field course in avalanche danger assessment. What's more, I was traveling the high country without an ice ax, not even a set of crampons. To safely navigate snow-laden mountains, both are essential tools. The ice ax is reminiscent of a compact pickax. It serves as a third leg for balance. And once the technique is mastered, it can be a lifesaver for arresting a fall. Crampons are steel-toothed grips that strap on to climbing boots. They enhance traction and security on icy slopes far beyond what Vibram boot soles offer.

Both are indispensable equipment, but I was equipped with neither. I was winging it, though only out of naïveté, not cockiness. Perhaps my faux pas could be forgiven, if I'd been with a climbing partner or two. But I wasn't.

As I stomped my way cross slope, I heard a sickening crack. A fissure sheered the snowfield just above and straight ahead of me. Instantly, I was being swept down the mountain in a whooshing froth of white. It was an unreal experience—upright one moment, floundering down the mountain the next.

I'd heard about avalanches. Maybe seen them on TV. Perhaps even read about mountaineers or skiers being swept to their deaths, buried alive until they suffocated. *Surely, this couldn't happen to me!*

Whisked away in a moment, there was no time for thinking, for plotting strategy. Certainly no time to contemplate what the final outcome might be. There was only the instinct and urgency to react.

There were more hazardous places I could have provoked a mass snowslide—inclines with steeper pitch and greater snow load—places I'd be rushed off a cliff and covered with nary a trace. By comparison, this slide was composed, an accelerating slow ride.

To stay on the surface, I recall flailing my arms and legs, reminiscent of my awkward childhood efforts at learning to swim. Because I was near the fracture line that started the slide, there wasn't a surging mass trying to overtake me from above. Chalk one up to good luck. If the load had been greater, I could never have resisted its pull, as when I was gathered up by a twelve-foot breaker along the coast of Hawaii, tumbled by its awesome, foaming power and dashed, as it broke over me, onto the beach, leaving me gasping for breath and my skin abraded as if by sandpaper.

As it gathered momentum, the snow's consistency became heavier—like mashed potatoes—demanding greater effort to keep my arms and legs from being swallowed by the snow.

Then I spotted it. Through the swirling haze, the slide was propelling me toward a solitary tree. My eyes locked on that tree as a drowning man's sight must lock on bobbing flotsam. In moments, I'd be arriving at and then plastered against a stout subalpine fir.

Firs make lovely, pyramidal Christmas trees. But ornamenting a tree wasn't what I had in mind. Rather than becoming my final destination, I thought this tree could be my salvation. In a flash, I resolved to grab it, lay a bear hug on its eight-inch-thick trunk when we met.

The slide was traveling just slow enough, its direction true enough, and I was just crazy or desperate enough to pull it off. I kicked and twisted onto my belly, quartering feet first down the grade. Thank goodness, both legs slipped by the trunk to one side. If they had straddled it, I may have become an instant alto. With one arm and then the other, I hooked the tree. Intense pain shot through my shoulders. Still, I held fast.

If the frothing snow, clutching with invisible hands, had continued any longer, my arms might have been ripped from their sockets and left strewn in the avalanche run out like the limbs stripped from innocent trees. I imagined the white menace admonishing me, "You started this; now gravity is your master. Come along, surrender to its power and rest forever in this empire of snow."

But I hugged that tree until the shuddering, frozen mass had passed and come to a halt below me. I was left slightly stunned in the ensuing silence, as if this encounter had never happened. And that's the way gravity does its work: swiftly, anonymously, and relentlessly tearing down that which the opposing forces of nature have created. Everything is temporary in steep country, when viewed over expanses of time. To casual visitors, the mountains seem eternal and perhaps unchanging. But sustained familiarity, fed by watchfulness, reveals their true personality. No rock remains firmly bedded, no tree endures, and most surely the gathered snow is ever changing. Each dynamic tapestry of mountain building is a relentless story of geological change over eons that's countered by wind and water erosion and the relentless pull of gravity, a power to which a mere mortal is a temporary plaything.

Once the shaking in my legs subsided, I crawled to a crouch, gathered myself, and staggered to my feet. All essential moving parts seemed to be working. Concluding I'd had enough excitement for the day, I angled down the snow-swept grade toward the trail in the canyon far below.

♠

It's said that experience makes the best teacher. In my subsequent four decades of mountain travel, never again was I whisked down a slope by runaway snow. I've had no perilous close calls—except for that one incident in an Idaho canyon while photographing mountain goats. A careless step on icy rock sent me into a controlled tumble down a ten-foot drop. In retrospect, a broken middle finger seems a minor injury, considering the possible outcomes.

But another memorable incident involved my newfound climbing companion—a friend of the canine variety.

It was the spring of 1974, the tail end of my first full winter living deep in the Bitterroot Mountains. The previous fall, my graduate program chairman, Dr. Bart O'Gara, and I trucked a slide-in camper four miles into Fred Burr Canyon. We off-loaded it near the end of a crude track—a human artifact that excluded the corridor from the Selway-Bitterroot Wilderness Area when the boundaries were demarcated in 1964. The route became impassable to wheeled vehicles from November into May. As snow buried the two-track, I resorted to snowshoes and skis to haul supplies and to conduct research on the canyon's mountain goats.

Although just seven feet long and a mere four feet high, the camper provided a cot, propane space heater, two-burner cookstove, and a solid roof over my head. It served as operational headquarters and refuge for me, and for the shrews that relentlessly infested the place.

With plush white fur and back eyes and nose, my new Samoyed pup was a squat mirror image of the cliff dwellers I studied and had come to admire. I named him Kamook. That translates as "dog" from the language of the Chinook Indian tribe, from whom Meriwether Lewis and William Clark had acquired a mountain goat hide as they traveled down the Columbia River in 1805. A breed bred for Arctic conditions, the fifty-five-degree temperature of my cramped camper proved too toasty for him. Kam preferred burrowing outside in the snow and then pawed at the door for his breakfast when I stirred to brew coffee.

When fourteen weeks old, he made his first trek to my winter camp—four miles beyond the end of the plowed road. At the age of four and a half months, he began trailing me up the goat cliffs. Not always fond of the places I scrambled to capture goats or to record their behaviors up close, I sometimes had to boost my timid companion up steep pitches, in his first weeks as a mountaineering dog.

April was still winter on Fred Burr's goat cliffs. Goats remained restricted to limited areas of their winter refuges on the south-facing canyon wall. As the snowpack began to recede, goats sometimes probed the lower elevations in search of the first new plant growth, thereby making them more easily observed and counted and also conducive to another aspect of my research.

It was early afternoon that I spotted a nanny—a female goat—perched high on a broad cliff ledge. I began planning a route for a stalk. My goal was to capture and place a radio collar on her. The radio's beeping signal would allow me to track her migration to the heights where she'd eventually spend summer.

To lay my hands on her would require an approach from downwind and out of sight, to the east. After a stout climb of some thousand feet of elevation and then a traverse to the west, the route would place me above where she was feeding. If all went as planned, I'd be in position to fire a dart into her rump from my capture gun. A well-placed shot would inject a drug that would shortly immobilize her. But everything had to go just right.

My intrepid companion joined me that day, faithfully following me up a steep debris chute. Beneath the northward-trending sun, the snow cover had compacted—softening to mush during the day and freezing rock hard at night. Kam carefully placed his feet in the tracks I punched. The melting snow slickened a clutter of slide rock beneath, making the footing all the more treacherous. Our assault of the thirty-degree slope was punctuated by some creative recoveries of missteps on my part and by a few plaintive pleas from my protégé to reconsider the mission. Even so, Kam trailed me like a shadow, bumping against my legs whenever I paused.

After an hour, we'd gained the necessary elevation. From there, we gingerly traversed the mountainside to the west and then descended to the anticipated vantage point above the nanny.

Many things can go wrong on these stalks, besides the chance of snapping an ankle or tumbling from a slick ledge. In more than two dozen attempts to dart goats, I succeeded in capturing but three. Several painstaking stalks found my quarry in a place where I dare not squeeze the trigger for fear that a magnificent animal would plunge to its death once the muscle-relaxing drug took effect. At the end of other roundabout approaches, my target had simply vanished—gone from the lofty perch where I'd spotted it earlier from the canyon bottom.

That was the upshot of this day's stalk. The nanny was nowhere to be seen—not on the ledge, not along the slope farther below. Just vanished, as if swallowed by the mountain. All I found were some tracks and clumps of raisin-shaped droppings studding a patch of snow, proving, sure enough, she had really been there. I felt that familiar pang of disappointment, with nothing to show for the effort but sweat-soaked clothes. I'd missed another chance to expand my knowledge about the travels of these mountain goats. Kam, on the other hand, couldn't have cared less. He'd collapsed in the shade, with his bushy tail wrapped across his face.

But I was an opportunistic field naturalist. In every failed capture attempt, I found a silver lining. Enough evening light remained to inspect the nanny's feeding site to learn which plants she'd been eating—another occasion to discover a bit more about this enigmatic beast's art of eking out a living where meals are scattered snacks on precarious shelves.

From the overlook where our stalk ended, I began working my way down the escarpment to the ledge beneath. Wrinkles in granite and cracks in the cliff served as handholds and places to jam the toes of my boots. I hugged the rock, moving only one limb at a time. Water trickled in sun-warmed places and glazed the rock in shaded spots. The descent demanded my full attention. Not until I reached the safety of the nanny's feeding site did I discover that my companion hadn't chosen to follow.

On a bleak slice of mountain thirty feet above me, Kamook the Wonder Pup protested pitifully.

"C'mon Kam. C'mon down. Let's go boy."

No encouragement could convince him that his life was not in peril. I followed the ledge left and then right, searching for a more agreeable route that he might be coaxed to descend. No such luck. With each attempt to start down the rock, as his front paws began to slip, he recoiled to the safety of the overlook. There he paced and whimpered inconsolably.

I saw no other choice. I rock climbed back up to where he yipped his approval. As if snatched from the jaws of death, he greeted me until I thought his wagging tail would come unhinged. If dogs could rationalize such situations, Kam probably thought his canine judgment had prevailed. His master reconsidered his obvious miscalculation and had come to hang with him until his puppy chow would magically appear.

But masters make no such foolish blunders, as any human will tell you. We were still five hundred feet up the mountain, night was closing in, and there was no more-economical route down from the ledge. With a length of parachute cord I kept stashed in my rucksack, I cinched a loop behind his front legs. The look in his eyes told all: the end must be near. Despite his protestations, I lowered him down, loosed the cord, and descended the escarpment as before.

The remaining trek to the camper was uneventful. After an extra cup of puppy chow, the day's trauma seemed to be forgotten. Kam chose to sleep with me in the camper that night.

Such events are life changing, even for a shaggy dog. Kamook became a more resourceful mountaineer. Never again did he require being slung on a cord down a cliff after that.

NINE

LIGHTNING

Electricity is really just organized lightning.
—George Carlin, *Napalm and Silly Putty*

My wife, Diana, tells me that I have no regard for lightning. She may have a point.

As we hunker against a block of granite with the sky rent by thunderbolts, I recall that she's suggested this before. The first time I took her fly-fishing, we had no more than waded into a local stream when thunderheads began billowing on the southwestern horizon. As so often happens, trout began to rise. Clouds of dusky caddis flitted above the water, like miniature marionettes dancing on a puppeteer's strings.

Those of us who are die-hard fly casters know that this can be a mesmerizing time. In fact, time stands still. We become consumed by the drama of emerging adult insects, fish rising in numbers and in pools where moments earlier there were none, and the rhythm of casting: feeding out line, adjusting the loop's trajectory to lay down the perfect cast. Finally the caddis or mayfly imitation that was so carefully tied last winter alights just three feet upstream from the very spot where that big fish just sipped his last snack. Set the hook, net, and release; then repeat the seduction once again.

"Bruce, that looks bad." Rather than assessing my technique, Diana was pointing toward a furious looking sky. She wasn't watching the bugs or the eddying current or the drift of her fly. She was holding the coils of her lime-green-colored five-weight line against the rod's cork handle. Our minds were in totally different places: mine, preoccupied just twenty feet in front of me; Diana's, anxiously fixed on the horizon. Just two rod lengths from each other, we were poles apart.

Despite the approaching storm, the wind had not yet come up to chase the swarming buffet away. The hatch and the feeding frenzy intensified.

I turned to my right, where she'd been casting, and found her edging toward the shore. I quickly retrieved my line and secured the elk hair caddis in the hook keeper. I would guide her into position, an ideal angle that would minimize leader drag. From there, odds were good she'd draw a strike from that seam in the current now peppered with rises. And then she'd land her first wild trout on a fly rod. This was the perfect moment. I could hardly wait to see the look on her face.

It was still early in our married life. Among the things I had yet to learn was that Diana had no use for testing her resistance to electrical current. Still, she's a cool customer; and when she'd tried redirecting my attention to the horizon, any hint of alarm in her voice just didn't register. Next time it did: "I think this is crazy, standing here in the stream waving sticks."

No exclamation point needed.

I came to my senses. Water is a good electrical conductor. Brandishing graphite lightning rods while immersed thigh-deep in it shows little regard for self-preservation. An image of a horse that I used to ride flashed before my eyes. He'd been struck dead at the edge of a pond—his face scorched and electrified. No opportunity to learn from that experience. Taking a drink when lighting carves the sky is very bad timing.

We left the stream as the first raindrops (more like small puddles) began pelting us. That first trout would have to wait. We'd fish another day.

Then there was the first time we visited a golf driving range, my effort to teach Diana the fine points of whacking a small white ball. After we spilled our two bucketsful onto the tee box and began swinging away—I swear, it wasn't ten minutes—a thunderstorm charged over the Gravelly Mountains, barreling headlong toward the Mountain Meadows Golf Course. I couldn't have picked a worse time for a first golf outing. I read *that* look in Diana's eyes. We gathered up the clubs and headed to the truck.

Here, at the summit of Prospector Peak, one of many ten-thousand-foot peaks in the mountain range behind our house, I understand the anxiety in her voice. I've shared Diana's queasy feelings when the sky turns greenish black and snuffs out the sun. From years of mountaineering and rock climbing, I've gained respect for storms on mountaintops that I obviously don't possess in the lowlands. I think the difference comes from a history of close calls.

One unsettling episode was on an exposed ridge (not unlike this one where Diana and I are pinned) in the high country of Wyoming. I had hiked to the top of an alpine ridge where I'd spotted some elk the day before. I wanted to observe the bunch of cows and month-old calves. After cresting the ridge, I eased down the other side until I spied them in a glade far below. Several cows were bedded in dappled sunlight beneath a scatter of conifers. Others casually cropped sprouting delicacies while their calves frolicked nearby. Some calves sprinted and dodged haphazardly, as though afterburners had been ignited. Two others butted heads in mock combat. Their white spots showed like sun drops on rusty flanks, as they jousted in an emerald meadow.

Unnoticed high above, I sat enjoying their playful behavior, until a change redirected my attention. Rushing from the Wind River Range's twelve-thousand-foot peaks to the west, a fierce bank of clouds was swallowing the afternoon sun. Before tucking the binoculars inside my parka, I glassed the little herd of elk a final time. Rumbling in the distance was punctuated by a thunderclap much closer. The elk seemed unfazed by the approaching storm; I began making tracks.

As I topped the ridge, the first wind-driven raindrops stung my face. The nearest cover was a huddle of whitebark pines a quarter mile away. I headed for their scant protection.

Lightning streaked and the trailing thunder rapidly closed the gap following each flash. Minutes later my arms were tingling. Pulling up my shirtsleeves, I was alarmed to see the hair twisting into punk spike hairdos. Static electricity engulfed me. A bolt blasted the ridge off to my left and belched an acrid electric smell that seared the mucous membranes of my nose.

That was enough! Upright, I was the tallest object on the ridge, though seldom had I felt punier. I ditched my binoculars and metal-framed daypack beneath a jutting, flat rock. I sprinted for shelter beside the only boulder within one hundred yards.

As quickly as it advanced, the storm bore east. Within fifteen minutes, I was standing in brilliant sunlight, transfixed by a dazzling double rainbow awash in drizzle from a cloudless sky. It was a scene from a fairy tale.

🌲

During my years among mountain goats, studying their lives and capturing their images on film, lightning seemed to follow me like a faithful companion. Several times I shed my camera and lenses, spotting scope and tripod and sprinted for cover. Such moments made me wonder how many of the mountains' wild residents do electrical discharges occasionally clobber? My time exposed to nature's ferocity pales compared to the life of a mountain goat, who spends twenty-four hours a day 365 days a year on cliffs and soaring ridges. How many goats have suffered deadly blows that go unrecorded by two-legged mountaineers? Such mysteries exemplify how much about life and death in the wilderness remains unknown to us.

Now, so many years later, Diana and I remain hunkered against a rock, no more than a pint-sized boulder. The rain pelting the hoods of our parkas fills each hiatus between clashes of thunder. Even if we dared to move, I see no better shelter across the alpine tundra. One storm cell after another keeps us pinned for forty-five minutes. Now as much as ever, I'm awed and humbled by its power as the storm's fury enfolds us.

Just moments before we scrambled to our provisional refuge, I was face down on the mountain as a thunderbolt crashed overhead. Perhaps it's because of vivid memories of past close calls or because at the roof of the world, lightning seems so near. But I know better. It happens still, from time to time, a trigger that's entrenched from my year in Vietnam. Incoming! Hit the deck!

♠

There was a night in Vietnam when I witnessed a special effects show, not an aerial salvo but a display solely of nature's doing. It was my turn on watch, three hours starting at midnight, listening and watching for Charlie. The other two members of my machine-gun team were fast asleep ten feet behind me in our hooch. (The hooch was two drab-green ponchos snapped together along one edge, supported down the middle by a ridgepole, and staked to the ground along two sides. With both ends open, wind-driven rain still soaked three marines packed like sardines beneath this makeshift shelter.)

I sat on the edge of our thigh-deep foxhole, peering into the night. By moonlight, I watched as clouds gathered above a line of hills on the horizon. The air took on a telltale smell. Monkeys chattered somewhere in the jungle. The night's tranquility was about to end.

During that year in Nam, there were plenty of stormy days and nights. But this one was different. The mountaintop where Kilo Company, my unit, had dug in for the night was nearly treeless. Artillery shells from an earlier bombardment had seen to that. From my top-row seat in this wildland arena, stretched a panoramic view across the rainforest canopy—a welcome reprieve from being enveloped in it. As the clouds charged closer, I expected everything to disappear in wind and rain and blackness. Instead, the cloud bank—laden with cold, moist air—plunged into the valley. Then the fireworks began.

Lightning blasted through the rolling, swirling blackness. Rather than brewing above, the storm boiled at eye level and below me, as if I were watching it from an aircraft. Streak after streak, every few seconds, illuminated the clouds from within. All the while, I was washed in moonlight, with only shreds of ragged clouds billowing up sporadically to obscure its glow. It was an eerie feeling that brought on a touch of vertigo.

Then in an instant, the mass of clouds swept upward along with the lightning. The storm overtook me, my unit, and the mountain. Scurrying figures lit up in blazing flashes clutched their hooches to save them from being sucked skyward like Dorothy and Toto. The next day, a chopper medevaced two marines who'd been partially paralyzed by a lightning strike inside our perimeter.

Forty-seven years later, only the most vivid details from my year in Vietnam do I recall, like that night's otherworldly thunderstorm. Some of the most poignant images, time has allowed me to block out. But there are others that I hang on to because they buoyed my spirits and reminded me of all the goodness in the world.

One such transcendent moment was a still night when the moon shone through slits in the forest canopy. It was my turn on watch.

Standing watch could be spooky and tense. Just keeping alert was demanding enough after a long day of ground pounding with fifteen pounds of gear on my back, fifteen more belted around my waist, and a thirty-one-pound machine gun balanced across my shoulder. If intel had reported enemy troop movements in the area or if the night crackled with nameless sounds—either real or imagined—it set the nerve endings on high alert.

On the flip side, it was the one occasion when I had uninterrupted time—time to think about home and those things that mattered most, and about what I'd do if I made it out alive. If there was moonlight, I'd sometimes scribble letters to family and friends. That familial connection and quiet introspection helped maintain perspective, and sanity.

That night, somewhere in the middle of Vietnam's nowhere, I was writing to my parents. The full moon seemed so close that with a poke of my pencil, I took a stab at adjusting the old man's smile. Moonlight was my ally, increasing the chances of spying Charlie's approach on silent feet. But it also illuminated my silhouette as I sat on the edge of the foxhole with the м60 across my lap.

The jungle was soundless. No wind to rustle leaves. No birds at oh dark thirty announcing daybreak. And no twigs snapping from who knows what. My mind had drifted to Michigan and friends and cars and college one day in Montana. Then I was snapped back to this foreign and unnerving place.

Somewhere in the jungle, I heard it once and then twice more. A roar. The roar of a tiger announcing his presence to others. His territorial trademark resonated through the jungle and stood the hair on my neck at attention. Then just silence. *I did hear it*, I told myself and later confirmed with others who'd been on watch at other positions. Nothing else that lived in this jungle could make that sound. That roar was confirmation. This was wild land still alive with fierce, wild creatures, despite all that years of carpet bombing, napalming, Agent Orange defoliation, and 2.6 million American forces had done to diminish that.

That feeling of being immersed in something that's primordial, enduring, and unrestrained—that's what captures the imagination of those of us who cannot live without wild places. Like towering mountains, ancient forests, free-flowing rivers, and solitude, lightning and the call of wild creatures remind us that nature is reluctant to relinquish its rule over wildlands. Decades later, the jungle has reclaimed the denuded and bomb-cratered landscape. I find humility and freedom in that.

In war-torn Vietnam, that roar of a tiger creased a smile on my face.

TEN

COLLECTING

Every child is a beginning explorer naturalist. Hunter, gatherer,
scout, treasure seeker, geographer, discoverer of new worlds, all
these are present at the child's inner core, rudimentary
perhaps but straining for expression.

—Edward O. Wilson, *The Creation*

Next to the fireplace, propped against a stone wall, is a magnificent souvenir from my time as a field biologist and backcountry traveler. It's the envy of many a hunter who has seen it, but it's not the only relic I've stumbled across and carted home in a backpack. More about this trophy by the fireplace in a bit.

Strewn elsewhere on shelves, walls, and desktops are skulls of mammals and birds, eggs (with the contents removed, of course), tanned hides, assorted feathers, and even the shed skin of a two-and-a-half-foot-long snake. These are the treasures gathered over the years by one who has spent way too much time in the mountains and rangelands to have developed more modish tastes in interior design. In a sense, these possessions are no different than the pretty things that most humans collect, display, and wear: curios, fine artwork, chic clothing, and jewelry. Bling seems fixed in our species' DNA.

Amazingly, my wife, Diana, who was born and raised in Brooklyn and spent most of her adult life in suburban New

Jersey, has become accustomed to all the "dead things," as she's wont to call them. That was not the case at first. When she moved to Jackson, Wyoming, where we met in 2003 and began the rest of our lives together, I recall her startled gaze when she first beheld the mountain goat head poking from the wall above my fireplace. But to my relief, and delight, she seems to have grown into her surroundings.

Perhaps it's a case of the novelty wearing off, the way some people overlook house clutter or adapt to happy crap in their yards. Rather, I choose to believe that she's come to really appreciate these artifacts of life around us—a testament to her love of the beauty of wild things as much as her tolerance of her husband's decorating quirks. Her volunteer work at national wildlife refuges and state parks left her no stranger to wild things and how they enrich our lives. She even volunteered to crawl into an active wolf den (*mano ý lobo*) to inspect it for pups. That was during a wolf-ecology field course she took in northern Minnesota. Her story is that she was the only class member slim enough to wriggle headfirst into the big dog's lair. But modest to a fault, she was rabbit quick to volunteer, I suspect.

Anyway, she accepts the bear, badger, and muskrat skulls and the elk hide and antlers. But she draws the line that none find their way into the rooms designed for sleeping and showering. No leering eyes or hollow eye sockets in rooms where clothes are shed.

Among the collection, her favorite item may be the massive buffalo skull that hangs on a living room wall. It's quite majestic, if I may say so myself, against a background of rustic barn wood we scavenged from a decrepit mining shack.

The weathered skull makes quite a conversation piece looming ten feet above the floor. Beyond the dome-shaped frontal bones; protruding, armored orbits; and flattened nasal bones, the fist-thick horns jut outward and curve upward, measuring twenty-nine inches across their outside spread. This was a big boy. His body mass may have tipped the scales at nearly a ton in the prime of his life.

Beyond its impressive appearance, the skull's discovery makes quite a story. It was one of those unforgettable days. An instance of pure serendipity, I went afield with no intention or even a thought of looking for such a historic treasure—something those with more urbane tastes might regard as just old, grubby bones.

I think the year was 1980, during the time I worked as the first wildlife biologist on the Wind River Indian Reservation. Several days before the hunting season opener, I was scouting for elk on a mountainside of the Shoshone National Forest, northwest of the reservation. The week's weather had been unseasonably warm and dry. Such weather dries out herbaceous vegetation, sapping nutritional content as carbohydrates are sucked into root systems. Primarily grazers, elk retreat to deep forests seeking better forage where the shaded soils retain some moisture. Cooler temperatures in the shade of forest canopies also make for easier living. I can relate. Ever since my years in Vietnam and the California Desert, I much prefer the cold to summer's heat.

Most elk frequent higher elevations at this time of year—September and early October. Cows and calves are still laying on body weight for the lean months of the coming winter. And the bulls are wherever the cows are found, as this is the breeding season, or rut. Being wise to their ways, from my time in Montana's and Wyoming's mountains, I headed high to find a good place to bag an elk when the hunting season opened next week.

Starting at over seven thousand feet of elevation, I hoofed my way upward through willow and alder thickets and mountain meadows studded here and there with the season's last wildflowers—purple coneflowers, showy asters, and sticky geraniums. But mostly I snaked through forested habitat—lodgepole pine and Douglas fir on the drier slopes and then, as the elevation increased and I wound onto a north-facing slope, a pristine spruce-fir forest. Some of these old soldiers were here long before Lewis and Clark made their epic 1804–1806 westward journey.

Beneath the trees lay a thick carpet of organic matter. At eight thousand feet, under the dense canopy of ancient forests, the twigs, needles, and cones of conifers decompose ever so slowly. Among them in the humus lives a vibrant community of bacteria, mycorrhizal fungi, invertebrates, and who knows what else that squirms and oozes, still undiscovered. Except for a careless step that snaps a dry branch, a hunter can walk almost soundlessly on this cushion of detritus. And I was a hunter that day, seeking elk or signs of their presence: freshly nipped grasses; hoof prints registered in moist soil; and most tellingly, the barrel-shaped droppings that signify the passing of ungulates.

Deer, moose, elk, and other animals each produce their own sized and shaped fecal pellets that advertise to the hunter which type of game passed by. The softer and darker the pellets, the more recently an animal made them. When very fresh—only a few hours old—the droppings of elk retain a dark-greenish cast, a reflection of the digested plants that compose them.

Deep in the forest, I began spotting these signs of recent elk activity. My pace slowed to a crawl as I inspected the spoor. As I bent low from time to time, life on the forest floor materialized everywhere: beetles; the shells of land snails; and the ubiquitous, scurrying microengineers of the earth's landscape—ants. I wondered for a moment how many species of these amazingly successful insects an expert like E. O. Wilson might identify here. To me, there were just three types: large black carpenter ants that gnaw dead trees into pulp, the tiniest brown ones, and others of in-between size.

I veered left to a particularly elky-looking stand of spruce where the grade of the mountain grew gentle along the shoulder of a ridge. This was the kind of place that elk seek to bed down, rest, ruminate, and consider where next to head.

I quickly came upon several heaps of fresh elk poop. But even before I spied their sign, I smelled the elk.

My hearing was fairly well shot, even then, some thirty-five years ago. Unprotected exposure to the sounds of war, including thousands of rounds fired from my machine gun during training and in combat, had taken a toll. On my return from Vietnam, the doctor who checked my hearing during my exit exam at El Toro Marine Corps Air Station measured the damage. At the conclusion of the test, in which each ear is subjected to a random series of tones, the doctor scribbled on a chart and then called for the next marine being discharged from active duty.

"Doc," I said, "how'd I do on the test?"

"You have the hearing of a sixty-year-old," he responded impassively.

Though sounds may escape me, I seem to have compensated with increased olfactory perception. Hiking and hunting with others, I'm generally the first one to smell any elk in the neighborhood. So what do elk smell like, you ask? To me, it's a barnyard-like smell, not offensive, but a rather sweet, musky aroma. It's distinctively elk and a sure sign that the animals have recently been in the vicinity.

Instinctively I stopped to listen (for all the good that usually does) and peer through the trees, expecting to spot vertical slices of tawny flanks or chocolate manes of animals. I also poked a finger into my mouth and held it up, judging on which side it first felt cool, as a slight breeze evaporated the saliva on the windward side. The source of the aroma lay in that direction.

I had just begun moving again, treading in stealth mode, taking extra care to avoid any branches with each step, when I saw it. Barely poking from the forest litter was a two-inch-long piece of bone.

To a field biologist, bones are more than a curiosity. Out of necessity as a lab instructor of a university mammalogy class, I became a quick study of bones and how each type differed in shape and size among groups and species of mammals. As the National Elk Refuge biologist, later in my career, I worked with dead animals as an everyday part of the job, investigating and performing necropsies on their remains. But even earlier, starting at the age of fourteen, my early training in how animals are put together and the proper means of taking them apart began with butchering beef, pork, lamb, chickens, and ducks, in my grandfather's butcher shop.

I'm drawn to bones I find afield, just as a botanist is drawn to petals and seeds. Besides discerning who once owned each bone I find, I'm curious about how old the animal may have been? Does it show signs of injury? Do other clues tell a story?

What I spotted in the Shoshone Forest was not a single bone. As soon as I kneeled beside it, I knew it was part of something much larger hidden in the ground. Over the next twenty minutes, I picked and pawed using my fingers and jackknife, gingerly excavating and sweeping away needles and humus and mineral soil. What initially was the size of a silver dollar grew into the full skull of an ancient buffalo, an American bison. Yes, truly ancient, because the last free-roaming bison in this area—and across most of their North American range—were decimated by Euro-Americans in the 1880s. Freed from its earthen grave, the remains of the animal I was holding had died a century or more ago. Like paleontologists seeking fossilized dinosaurs or oceanic adventurers combing the seas for Spanish doubloons, uncovering an antiquity, if only a skull, is a chance to touch and admire a piece of the past.

Not only was the entire skull intact (minus the lower jaw), but remarkably, both horn sheaths were anchored on their cores of bone that grew from each side of the skull. Remarkable indeed, because the horn sheaths—the part of the horn that we see on a live cow or sheep or goat, and the part that continues to grow in length and thickness over time—typically deteriorate far faster than true bone. Like our own fingernails and hair, the sheaths are composed of keratin. When people unearth the skulls of long-deceased bison, it's only the bleached bone that typically remains. Though the outer layers were eroding, the horn sheaths remained attached full-length to the tips. Because of its state of preservation, this skull was a treasure to behold.

Leaving clumps of soil attached for more meticulous removal at home, I wrapped the skull in my jacket and strapped it to the outside of my rucksack. There was no way it could fit inside. On the two-mile hike back to my truck, I couldn't stop thinking of my good luck. Making the day all the more memorable, I found parts of two more bison skulls while hiking out.

But the best memory, and the real treasure, is being out in the wild. The things collected along the way are just reminders of roaming across wildlands, just as photographs help us remember our experiences. A bison skull is just more substantial.

After transferring from the Wind River Indian Reservation to the National Elk Refuge, I made acquaintance with a paleontologist at the University of Wyoming. I described the skull I'd collected, and asked if he'd be able to tell how old it was. On a business trip to the university, I left it at his office. From a physical examination, he concluded that it was likely 150 years old. The 1830s. Dating it to the time of Jim Bridger, Jeddediah Smith, and the heyday of the fur-trapping era. This was a time when millions of bison still roamed the continent and Shoshone and Crow Indians would have hunted them near this skull's resting place. Maybe that's how the bison met its end—a feast for a tribal gathering, the robe sheltering a family in their teepee. This wasn't a *T. rex* I'd unearthed; but given the history of bison in the West, this was a piece of times gone by to be preserved.

If I wanted, my paleontologist colleague said he could date it more precisely. Radiocarbon dating, based on radioactive decay of the carbon-14 isotope in organic matter, could decipher if the bison had died more than 150 years ago, which he doubted. Aside from the hefty fee to do so, I decided 150 years, give or take a decade, was good enough for me. At the root of my love of the biological sciences are the unending mysteries in nature. Never knowing all the answers is part of the allure.

♣

And then there's that trophy I mentioned back in the opening to this chapter, the one in our living room next to the fireplace. Now that's a story that deserves some telling, partly because of the human nature aspect of the collecting.

In June 1977 I'd landed my first permanent job with the U.S. government as a wildlife biologist. The Bureau of Land Management—which manages more acres of federal land than the U.S. Forest Service, Fish and Wildlife Service, or National Park Service—hired me as the Indio Resource Area biologist in the California Desert. Among my responsibilities, I was charged with developing a habitat management plan for the Santa Rosa Mountains.

If you've not heard of this thirty-mile-long range in Southern California, you've likely heard of the towns of Palm Springs, Palm Desert, and Rancho Mirage rimming the range's eastern flank. Besides movie-star retreats and dozens of golf courses cleared of mesquite and cultivated from the sand, the area is famous for its thriving desert bighorn sheep population, at least thriving in the late 1970s. The plan's focus was on conservation of those sheep and a few quite rare, endemic species of the Santa Rosas, such as the desert slender salamander.

Up to this time, I'd bounced from Montana to Wyoming to Washington and back again. I no more than settled into a new rental dump than each four- to five-month seasonal job would end. Like politicians who begin campaigning after reelection, I was perpetually mailing off job applications to stay employed as a biologist, until the BLM offered me permanent employment.

The first week I arrived in California, I met the local biologist for the California Department of Fish and Wildlife. Vernon Bleich was a sharp twenty-something who'd recently graduated with a master's degree from California State University, Long Beach. His supervisor was a longtime desert rat who was intimately familiar with the Santa Rosas and their sheep. A curmudgeonly sort, Bonnar Blong eyed me at our introduction with a heaping dose of suspicion. Montana. Wyoming. Washington. What did I know about the desert? I'd never set foot there before. Sure, I'd studied mountain goats, but that was a far cry from his beloved desert sheep.

Nonetheless, Bonnar offered to begin my desert education with a week in the Santa Rosa Mountains. The state would charter a helicopter to drop the three of us at some far-flung location of the sheep range. Over the course of the next five days, we'd backpack and camp, winding twenty-some miles from seven thousand feet of elevation to a vehicle dropped for us at a spot just above sea level.

To develop a habitat management plan for the Santa Rosas, I needed to develop a map of its plant communities. This week would give me a great start. As we worked our way down the ridges and canyons, mapping plant communities on topographic maps, I'd soon learn that changes in elevation—and therefore temperatures and precipitation—create a complex mosaic of habitat types.

So two weeks after I arrived in Southern California, Bonnar, Vern, and I—along with tents, sleeping bags, food, and all manner of field gear—were plopped on a lovely flat spot (one of the few that could accommodate a chopper landing) with a view east nearly to the Colorado River.

The first day was a personal crash course on desert plant identification. I scribbled notes in my plant field guide as Bonnar pointed out the number of petals and stamens, leaf margin patterns, microsite preferences, and other key details of the flora. He also advised me to steer clear of a plant sardonically called teddy bear cholla (or jumping cholla). From a distance, it looks like a fuzzy, soft plant with short branches resembling a teddy bear's arms. But looks are deceiving. Close up, that fuzziness is a solid mass of formidable, barbed spines. This was the plant world's equivalent of the spitting cobra, I came to believe.

"All you gotta do is get close, and it will find you!" Bonnar warned.

Work during summer in the desert starts at first light, to accomplish as much as possible before the sun begins frying flesh. The plan was that we'd each hike and map predetermined geographic areas each day. Now a certified desert "veg expert," I was entrusted to carry my weight in mapping the botanic landscape. We'd meet back at camp by midday, by the time the sun had sent the lizards underground.

It was rough country with no straight path anywhere. Weaving through scattered rock, shrubs, and cactus required focusing on every step. A misstep could roll an ankle and send an inattentive hiker headlong into one of those bloodthirsty chollas. Bad enough the pain, but the embarrassment of needing spines plucked from my backside would do my untested reputation no good.

This wonderland of unfamiliar geology, red-blooming Ocotillo trunks (like octopus tentacles reaching for the sky), and strange beetles, reptiles, and birds overwhelmed yet fascinated me with its variety. According to the list that Bonnar had handed me, I did my best to stay focused on sketching out the plant associations.

Late morning, I took a break. Easing onto a large boulder, I dropped my daypack and began to scan the canyon wall a half mile beyond me for those elusive sheep—animals the same color as the backdrop. I was looking for movement that would disrupt their disguise—maybe the flash of a cream-colored rump against the brown and buff-colored rocks. No luck.

I lowered the binoculars, now panning the slope below me. Something caught my eye. Something that looked out of place, not part of the jumbled rocks and shrubs studding the landscape. I marked its location, hoisted my pack, and headed down. Shortly, I was standing, dumbfounded, beside the full skeleton of a bighorn sheep. It was a ram, and a big one.

The skull lay with both horn sheaths beside it. They had slipped off the horn cores as the connective tissue decomposed. My first urge was to shout, "Yee haaa!" My second was to return the horn sheaths to the skull to see how impressive he looked. They slipped on perfectly.

Viewing the head from the side, a ram whose horn tips curl far enough to come in line with the base of the horn at the skull is considered a full curl. Full-curl bighorns are uncommon, in part because old sheep (ones who've lived long enough to produce that much growth) broom their horns, rubbing and braking down the tips, presumably so they don't obstruct peripheral vision. This one was just short of full curl, a seven-eighths-curl ram; and his horn tips were unbroomed, the horns perfectly symmetrical. I couldn't wait to show Bonnar and Vern this majestic find!

I looked around as though they'd have heard my whoop and come running—probably expecting to find me impaled on a cactus or fallen into a ragged ravine. Of course there was no one in sight. No one calling out my name. The others were rambling out of earshot from me.

My eyes returned to the sheep. Surely this must be unusual, I mused, to find a dead bighorn. There were just five hundred in the whole mountain range, and the chances of finding the remains of one in this convoluted country must be infinitesimally small.

I knelt down and felt the series of ridges and grooves notched in the tawny, curved horns. I counted the annular rings, one laid down each year when growth ceases during the leanest time of year. In northern populations of sheep, such as Rocky Mountain bighorns or Dall thinhorn sheep, growth ceases in winter when food quality is spare. But in southwestern deserts, rings are laid down during the blazing heat of summer. A ten-to twelve-year-old ram is an old one. Some lucky ones last a few years more. I counted six rings on this one's horns. A ram that should have been in his prime. Perhaps he'd left his genes behind in a few offspring that now strengthened the population.

I slipped the sheaths from his skull and tucked them in my pack. With a length of parachute cord, I tied the skull on top of the pack. Before leaving, I examined the remaining bones for signs of why this sheep had died. No bone breaks or compromised teeth. Nothing apparent. Another mystery without clues for solving.

I hoisted the pack to my back. It was more awkward than heavy. I would learn later that the skull and horns together weighed seventeen pounds.

🌲

I was the first to arrive back at our camp. By the time Vern wandered in sometime past midday, my excitement had waned a bit. I'd put the sheaths back on the skull and propped it against a rock near the fire ring.

"Holy shit. Where'd you get that?" Vern exclaimed.

"A couple of miles that way," I pointed and related how I'd stumbled upon the skeleton.

When Bonnar traipsed in a bit later, he looked stunned upon spying the big skull. He seemed less than enthusiastic that I'd found it. As the afternoon wore on and the conversation bounced from our explorations and findings that day to the sheep skull, to what birds we'd seen, to the sheep skull, to the sparse amount of sheep sign (tracks and pellet groups), and back to the sheep skull, I was schooled by Bonnar about California law. That skull was not mine to keep. It belonged to the state of California. I'd have to surrender it when we returned to Riverside.

"Where?" I asked. Probably to the university, he thought. He would take care of that. I became convinced that I'd only have this treasure—a remarkable start to my desert biologist career—for the next three days as I packed it, along with my other gear, to our next camps and out of the mountains.

Vern had said little when Bonnar raised the subject of ownership. I just wrote that off as Bonnar being his senior and more savvy about such things. But by the time we reached the pickup truck, I'd had a chance to mull this over. I'd decide that Bonnar seemed a little too eager to relieve me of the sheep head.

When we pulled up to the BLM office late Friday, I thanked them both profusely for arranging the trip and for all the knowledge they had freely shared with me. It had been a five-day crash course in desert ecology. And I think that they were pleased with their student's aptitude.

I slung my backpack over one shoulder and headed toward my car.

"Hey, you forgot to leave that sheep," Bonnar shouted.

"I know," I called back to him. "I just want to take it home so my wife can see it."

The upshot of the tale is that no one at our BLM office was aware of a law that required someone finding sheep remains on public land to turn them in. Two or three weeks later, I drove to Idyllwild, a quaint town nestled in the San Jacinto Mountains, to meet up with Bonnar at his home. We were heading back into the Santa Rosas with other agency personnel and volunteers to do the annual census of bighorns in the Santa Rosas. We would all rendezvous in the Coachella Valley, get some instructions on protocols, and then scatter. We'd hike in pairs to assigned water holes that sheep regularly visit during the summer when water is scarce.

After our greeting in the driveway, Bonnar pointed to an old barn and said, "There's something I want to show you."

When he flicked on the light switch, the windowless walls of the barn wood came to life. As I swiveled my head from one side to the next, bighorn sheep were everywhere. More than a dozen skulls hung from spikes in the walls. Some had horn sheaths; others did not. Just like the bison skull I found years later, the sheaths decompose faster than bone or separate from the cores and fade into the desert sand.

In that moment, it struck me why Bonnar had wound his ruse about how I couldn't keep my sheep. He was a tad jealous. I was a neophyte, no more than a first-time visitor to the country that he knew better than most. Yet I had found a bighorn head superior to any that he'd collected during countless days afield. I'd not *earned* that big head. I think he initially wanted it for himself.

Bonnar Blong was a man who spent his life learning about bighorns and trying to conserve their dwindling numbers. He was a dedicated conservationist. He also took pride in being the local bighorn expert—the authority on all things sheep. But more fundamentally, Bonnar just loved bighorns, a dyed-in-the-wool sheep fanatic. Showing me his collection was his way of accepting me into that fraternity, despite my brief tenure in the desert. At least that's what I told myself.

Not once that day, nor anytime thereafter, did he mention the bighorn ram that I'd found in his Santa Rosa Mountains.

ELEVEN

OLD GARBAGE GUT

> Horses were never wrong. They always did what they did
> for a reason, and it was up to you to figure it out.
> —Jeannette Walls, *Half Broke Horses*

Among the rewards of being a wildlife biologist are the times spent working in wildlands. The big, raw landscapes of the northern Rockies, where wildlife easily outnumber humans, offer the space for large mammals to roam and relatively intact communities of flora and fauna to persist.

To accomplish my studies, where travel routes often were game trails, rather than roads, I flew 3,800 hours in helicopters and fixed-wing aircraft and hiked and backpacked thousands of miles during my career. But few days afield stuck in my memory like those traveling on horseback. My education with equines began on the 2.2-million-acre Wind River Indian Reservation, while helping the Shoshone and Arapaho people recover their wildlife heritage. My earliest riding days were backcountry trips to observe up close and learn about the reservation's varied habitats and wildlife.

During July 1978, two months after beginning my new job, I had my first look at reservation elk from the ground. I was on a horse pack trip deep in the backcountry of the Wind River Mountains to inventory the fish populations of high mountain lakes. These fish-sampling excursions, engineered by biologist Dick Baldes, were eagerly anticipated by him and our field station's other fisheries biologist, Reg Reisenbichler. I was excited to be invited on this high-country adventure, my first horse-pack trip ever.

Our destination was a cluster of lakes nestled at the headwaters of a Wind River tributary. In 1938 the tribes and the Secretary of Interior set aside a 180,387-acre roadless area in the high country of the reservation's Wind River Mountains, one of the most scenic ranges in the lower forty-eight states. This was a visionary achievement, predating our nation's Wilderness Act by twenty-six years. It permanently protected a pristine, glaciated landscape of subalpine meadows, virgin forests, over two hundred lakes, crystalline streams, and peaks soaring above twelve thousand feet. It also provided a haven for reservation wildlife.

Midmorning, we arrived at the trailhead . . . more accurately, where the road became too muddy and steep to pull horse trailers any farther. We saddled up, cinched the Decker packsaddles onto two of the horses, and loaded the canvas panniers. Loading a packhorse was as foreign to me as ballroom dancing, so I mostly observed and handed the others whatever they needed.

"Toss me those sleeping bags."

"That green stuff sack of clothes."

"Now the griddle. No, damn it! Don't toss that!"

"Now that picket."

"What?"

"The picket."

"Ummm."

"Over there. That steel pin with the long rope attached! Haven't you ever packed a horse before?"

I thought we covered that during my job interview, I mused.

After making sure fishing rod cases, sleeping pads, and other odd-shaped stuff was secured beneath the manti tarps and after wedging a trail saw and ax securely beneath lash ropes, we plopped onto the pickup tailgates for a snack before heading out. I passed around a bag of chocolate chip cookies, trying to make amends for not knowing what a picket was. When they came back to me, I took another and set the bag behind me in the pickup bed. Over our deliberations about whether we'd be camping on snow tonight arose a hideous coughing behind me. My designated saddle horse—a parrot-faced, barrel-bellied roan named Chippewa—was trying to extricate a plastic bag from his mouth. The same bag that moments before contained a dozen chocolate chip cookies.

"Git that away from him!" Dick chided.

I latched onto the horse's halter and wrenched the shredded, saliva-soaked bag from his mouth . . . *sans* cookies.

"That horse will eat anything! If he sees it and thinks it's food, he'll eat it." Dick chuckled.

"Can't be good for him," Reg chimed in.

As we joked about the thousand-pound food Hoover, Dick noticed a bag flapping on the ground next to the truck he and Reg were perched on. There lay a half-empty five-pound bag of red potatoes. No one had noticed them missing during the bustle of packing.

"By God, I told you he would eat anything!" Dick howled.

We all made a pass around the vehicles, seeking half-devoured produce, steaks, or toothpaste scattered in the grass or stomped in the mud. Finding none, we assumed "Garbage Gut," as he became known, had destroyed the evidence. We'd learn what else he'd dispatched by its absence when we unpacked the panniers at camp. As it turned out, Chippewa was just getting warmed up with surprises.

We locked the trucks and mounted up. Dick headed out, followed by Reg, each leading a packhorse. I'd been on a horse just enough times to say I had ridden, so the greenhorn brought up the rear. Not fifty yards from the vehicles was a large snow patch maybe two feet deep in the middle. Dick and Reg circled around, but my horse just headed straight for it. I reined him left, but he wouldn't be turned. In a moment, he lumbered onto the still-frozen patch, dropped to his knees, and without hesitation . . . rolled onto his side.

Man, I didn't see that coming! Just before my right leg would have been trapped beneath, I pitched myself free of the saddle. Sprawled on the snow, the horse rolled beside me, wearing a self-satisfied expression it seemed.

As the laughter up ahead subsided, I gathered myself, coerced the beast back to his feet, and led him off the snow. Whether he'd gotten vapor locked from the spuds or just wallowed for pleasure, I can't say. I can say I was both wary and pissed at the horse. Without looking at my companions, I wiped snow from the saddle seat with a bandana, straightened the saddlebags, and checked the cinch. Muttering a few choice words to which the others cackled, I remounted and began the trip again. This time with a very short rein on Garbage Gut!

Backcountry trails on the Indian reservation were sparsely traveled, largely because non-Indians could only "trespass" on reservation lands for purposes of fishing in designated areas. Most Shoshones and Arapahos didn't venture into the Wind River backcountry. Thus, riding the trails required clearing the trails.

We were obviously the first on this ten-mile stretch of rock, mud, and blowdown this season—something we carped about and yet we enjoyed having the place to ourselves. Early July is late spring in the Rockies. The trail repeatedly vanished beneath crusted snow as we passed the nine-thousand-foot contour line. Our horses would hesitate and then plunge into the snow with further prodding. When they floundered and stood miserably, we'd dismount and encourage them through. The afternoon's wet snow balled beneath the horses' feet, clung in frozen clods to their fetlocks, and soaked our pants.

That was the worst of it for Dick and Reg. I, on the other hand, was supervising a horse that found satisfaction in showing me who was in charge. Once, he veered off the trail, nearly scraping me out of the saddle on a stout pine. I grew ever more suspicious of his intentions. If a horse is capable of rational thinking, I'd say he had designs on ridding himself of a rider.

For a horse that wallowed in the first snow he encountered earlier, he now reacted quite differently. He seemed unfazed by shallow snow, but hesitated to follow Reg's saddle and pack-horse when the depth measured a couple of feet or more. Gently heeling his sides, offering encouraging words, and dispensing love pats between his ears only persuaded him to toss his head and jerk the reins through my grip. Perhaps he didn't decode those pats as loving.

Thinking it would facilitate the process of moving him along, I dismounted to lighten his burden. Leading Chip by the knot I'd tied in the end of his reins, I crossed a narrow band of snow. I was nearly across the drift when I was all but buried in horse-flesh. My hesitant mount had leaped forward, blasting his head into my back.

Since my time at the Wind River, I've ridden other horses with that same annoying habit of leaping over objects: logs, small creeks, and ditches. One horse had an aversion to nondescript muddy spots in a trail. He dodged around or leaped headlong across, as if each were the entrance to a bottomless black hole. Better be a fully engaged rider on that pony, or I'd find myself looking up at the south end of a horse headed north.

For self-preservation, Chip and I came to an understanding by midafternoon. If he wouldn't try broad jumping snowbanks—and me in the process—I wouldn't discuss his ancestry. There's an old saying: "Keep your friends close and your enemies closer." At the risk of sounding unkind, this advice helped me survive that knucklehead. I began shortening my grip on the reins and walking next to his head, all the while whispering insincere nothings to divert his bad intentions. I also used the ploy of telling him I had more cookies to share, if he behaved. To that comment, I swear I saw his ears jerk to high alert.

Man and beast had made a pact. The trail ride (and walk) was more bearable after that. If anyone tells you that horses don't understand the spoken word, I beg to differ. A day with Chip will adjust your thinking.

Late afternoon we reached our destination, the first in a chain of glacier-carved lakes. Its waters were veiled by ranks of dark firs and spruce—like soldiers standing guard at their posts. Half encircling the far shore rose rival ramparts ground smooth under Pleistocene ice. We topped a final rise holding the lake's dark waters in check. Their glassy reflections of talus and peaks and cumulus billows adrift in an azure sky were hypnotic. There was an unspoken consensus that this was the place to make camp.

The snow formed an undulating carpet, littered with pine needles, cones, and twigs. Refrigeration for the perishables would be no problem over the next week. Beneath breaks in the forest canopy, the snow had surrendered to the sun's radiant heat, exposing mats of sedges and grouse whortleberry shrubs. To a wall tent–sized spot of bare ground, we reined the horses. Then the unpacking began.

But first I led Chippewa to the driftwood-littered shoreline. I took a moment to just soak in the scenery and allow my knees to recover from stirrup strain. On the far ridge to my left, the one place gentle enough to cultivate an alpine meadow, a thin line of specs angled toward the skyline. Raising the binoculars slung round my neck, I watched seven rusty bodies trimmed in chocolate manes and ginger rumps melt into the sky.

I remember this image perfectly, for perfect it was. The first reservation elk I'd seen, not from the vantage point of a droning Cessna's cramped seat, but standing nearly ten thousand feet above sea level and ten miles deep in the Wind River Mountains . . . beside my trusty horse, Chippewa. Back to reality and the tasks that lay at hand. The horse tossed his head, tugging the reins through my gloved hand. Garbage Gut sensed dinner being unpacked.

♠

Following my work at the Wind River, my career took me two hours west to the National Elk Refuge in Jackson Hole, Wyoming. The refuge, you may know, is famous for the largest winter concentration of elk in North America. The spectacle of seven thousand to eight thousand animals gathered beneath the Teton Mountain Range is an artifact of human intervention, not a natural phenomenon. As numbers of elk on the continent plunged—as did populations of all other large mammals more than a century ago—the decision was made to rescue Jackson Hole's elk by feeding them in winter at what would become one of our earliest national wildlife refuges in 1912.

Over time, habit became tradition. And tradition became culture: a source of pride for the community of Jackson, Wyoming, and an economic driver of its tourist-based economy. For more than a century, the elk have been gathered and fed in numbers rivaling the human population of the adjacent town. This peculiar management program has maintained large numbers of elk, enabling some to survive to the advanced age of twenty or thirty. Even nearly toothless wonders can gum the high-protein alfalfa pellets delivered to them each winter.

As a nostalgic holdover from yesteryear—when the elk were fed baled hay from horse-drawn sleds, rather than diesel-powered behemoths—the refuge maintains a half dozen horses. They serve as conveyance for refuge staff to haze elk from the refuge in spring back toward summer pastures. They also take dignitaries on show-me trips of the refuge's northern hills. I used them also for wilderness travel in my field studies. The refuge provided an easy life, until each had his teeth floated and his hooves trimmed for the last time.

In winter, we turned them out on the refuge to feed among the elk. That was before a growing herd of bison, which spends winter on the refuge with the elk, began poking holes in the more dim-witted four-leggeds. For their safety, we began confining the horses to a fenced pasture in the mid-1980s.

On a Monday that followed a week out of town, I drove to the pasture to check on the horses. After many rides and pack trips over the years on a collection of steeds, what a surprise awaited me. As if he'd descended from celestial bluegrass pastures, where horses must go for their final grazing, I recognized an old friend—one I had assumed had already passed on.

Spend time with an animal and you don't forget its mannerisms, its looks, and of course its name. Some horses earn several handles over a lifetime of service to their owners. I worked with one refuge employee who had the same name for every horse he ever rode: old son-of-a-bitch. Not a fan of the equine breed.

In the pasture were the refuge horses that I rode and came to know: Bud, Mich, Red, and Dan. Standing among them that Monday was another I instantly recognized as Chippewa. I rubbed his graying, Roman-nosed head; and it seemed he recognized me too from my years at Wind River Reservation. As he nosed the empty palm of my glove, I felt sure he remembered a former connection we had nearly a decade before. Made me wish I had a cookie to share.

TWELVE

IN THE TIMBER

Of course, no man is entirely in his right mind at any time.

—Mark Twain, *The Mysterious Stranger*

Nature abounds with mysteries. The search to unravel these is among the reasons that wildlife research appeals to me. In a wildland laboratory, the interplay among species of wild animals, the varied places they live, and the vagaries of weather thicken the plot. In the Rocky Mountain West, an added element of danger helps keep tedium at bay, as was the case on June 5, 1990.

Ken Clegg and I were tethered to the blue telemetry receiver like horses tied to a hitching rail. Ken rotated the receiver's dials to tune the radio signals listed on the data sheet: Elk #1 167.381 MHz, #2 167.510 MHz, etc. The black reins of our headphones transmitted the beeps.

I was training Ken, a wildlife biology major at Utah State University, in the technology of wildlife radiotelemetry. He had been pumping gas and changing tires at a local service station for the summer when he learned of my project and offered to volunteer on his days off. Like dozens of others who offered their services to build their résumés or just to participate in wildlife studies, Ken was highly motivated, eager to contribute, and never failed to show for an early-morning session of remotely locating elk. Today was his first day on the job.

As he tuned each radio frequency, Ken rotated the twelve-foot-tall antenna mast with an attached crossbar resembling stubby bicycle handlebars. Once a signal's beeping was heard, two questions needed answering. At what compass bearing was the signal's volume strongest—a matter of deliberately adjusting the antenna's direction and recording the indicated bearing on a compass rosette—and was the animal still alive?

On top of my duties as the National Elk Refuge's biologist, I had embarked on a graduate degree program in 1988. I was piling it higher and deeper, as some translate the acronym of a PhD degree. On June 5 I was a month into the first field season of a three-year investigation of survival of newborn elk calves in northwest Wyoming. Along with my coworkers Billy Helprin and Alan Strassler, Ken and I were in the thick of the four-week period when some three thousand calves would be born to the elk of Jackson Hole.

Billy, Al, and I had captured and radio-collared thirty-five calves since the twenty-fifth of May. All were still "on the air," meaning the expandable radio collars we had fitted around their necks were functioning in active mode, pulsing at fifty beats per minute. When Ken tuned in elk number 20 on the list, a five-day-old calf when captured on May 30, I felt a mini adrenalin rush. Number 20's radio was pounding out one hundred beeps per minute—a mortality signal.

Straightaway I called Billy and Al on my two-way radio.

"Billy, have you tuned in number 20 yet?" I asked.

"Yeah, a few minutes ago. Why?"

"We just heard it on mortality mode. How about you?" I summoned.

"No, let me check it again," came his reply.

The double-fast beat throbbing from our receiver abruptly braked to fifty beeps per minute. "What's that mean?" Ken asked.

Before I could answer, Billy's voice crackled on the two-way radio: "Weird. When I tuned in again, it was beeping on mortality. Then it changed back to active mode."

"Same here," I replied. "Only two possibilities. Either the radio's malfunctioning, or we've got a dead elk."

I had instructed Telonics—the manufacturer of our radio collars—to incorporate a mortality switch into each collar's radio transmitter unit. The switches were programmed with a five-hour delay. Based on an ongoing study by my colleague Francis Singer in Yellowstone National Park and my own knowledge of their behavior, I reasoned that newborn elk could not remain perfectly still for five hours. Any motion at all would reset the mortality switch and keep the transmitter functioning on active mode for another five hours. Only if the collar, and presumably its wearer, were motionless for five hours would the double-fast pulsing alert me to investigate.

"I heard you guys talking," Al's voice boomed on the radio, the walkie-talkie we each carried to communicate. "I didn't hear number 20 on mortality."

"I have the feeling something disturbed it after laying still for barely five hours," I responded. "I'm going to check it out while you guys finish tracking the other radios." Locating each radio required triangulating the azimuths recorded at each of three tracking stations. Billy and Al's tracking stations were each nearly an hour's hike and drive away, and there were still more elk to track that morning.

"Sure you don't want someone to come along?" Al questioned and was echoed by Billy with matching anticipation.

"That's alright. It might just be a false alarm," I answered, wondering if Billy and I had both imagined what we heard. "I'll radio park dispatch with fifteen-minute welfare checks. If something comes up, I'll give you a call."

Of the 164 newborn elk we would capture and radio-collar over three years of study, number 20 was our first data point in deciphering two of the study's objectives: What was the rate of loss of calves during their first month of life? And of those that died, what were the causes of their demise?

Before I left Ken, I entered number 20's azimuths. The laptop triangulated a nearly perfect intersection a mile north in Timbered Island. At dusk, elk leave the shade of this densely forested lateral moraine in the park's central valley to graze the surrounding sagebrush grasslands. Luckily, from the inside-park highway, I'd have little more than a half-mile hike to number 20's location.

Before leaving my pickup at the shoulder of the park's interior roadway, I went through a mental list of protocols and equipment I'd need. National Park Service two-way radio: check. Telemetry receiver and antenna: check. Skinning knife: check. Large plastic bags: check. Necropsy kit: check. The latter included the tools of the trade to collect and preserve tissues from the remains of an animal.

After weaving through a swath of thigh-high sagebrush to reach Timbered Island, I began picking my way through the trees and downfall, on high alert. Noting the strength of the signal that pulsed from the receiver slung from my shoulder, I followed the searching arc of my antenna, a compact, three-element, handheld aluminum unit. Working into the heart of this island of old-growth lodgepole pine and Doug fir, half a mile wide by two and a half miles long, my anticipation grew. The signal beat like a heart from the depths of this dimly lit, temperate jungle. But when I paused for a moment, the radio's message was clear. The signal was modulating. The strength of the beeping that reached my ears was changing. That could only mean that the collar was moving.

As I zigzagged and clambered over corpses of fallen arboreal giants, the hair of my neck prickled. A trickle of sweat traced down my spine. This was not only the kind of dank hideaway favored by elk but also a clandestine lair where their predators retreat during midday.

My audible link to the elk continued to modulate. I grew more certain I wouldn't find a fidgeting calf at the signal's source. Two minutes more and I confronted a colossal, downed Doug fir before me. By now, I had turned the receiver's volume dial almost to zero as the beeping intensified. *The collar must be just beyond the log.* Rather than advance any closer, I chose to circle the apparent location of the collar. As I neared the tangle of roots where the giant had heaved from the ground, a huge head rose above a jumble of smaller logs not fifteen yards ahead. *Whoa! Get out the pepper spray!*

"Bear spray," as it's popularly called, is a highly effective repellant for deterring attacks by bears, mountain lions, and aggressive domestic dogs. Housed in a pressurized sixteen-ounce canister, the propelled capsaicin pepper causes violent inflammatory reactions. Used correctly, this nonlethal self-defense incapacitates an attacker by causing temporary blindness and irritation of respiratory mucous membranes. Works great on people too, so the sprayer needs to check the wind direction to avoid becoming a sniveling, well-seasoned target for a provoked predator.

Like any defensive weapon, it's only effective if actually on hand to use. As I reached for the holstered cylinder on my belt, I knew instantly where it was—in the equipment locker at my office.

When I embarked on this study, I'd crafted a raft of operational and safety protocols to cover each aspect of the field research: how to capture calves on horseback and from helicopter, flight procedures and coordination with Grand Teton Park's rangers and dispatcher, protocols for monitoring calves with radiotelemetry, and procedures for investigating and retrieving dead calves or parts thereof. I never seriously considered carrying a firearm (or seeking certification to do so). I was studying predation and other causes of mortality. Shooting a lion or bear would be no different than purging a disease agent. Such imprudence would alter the study's outcome, violate ethical standards of conducting wildlife research, and may preempt my obligation to exercise due caution in the field. A handgun or rifle would serve no justifiable purpose, particularly in Grand Teton and Yellowstone National Parks, where all wildlife is protected. Bear repellant; welfare radio checks to park dispatch; and a commonsense approach about whether, when, and how to investigate each mortality site were my chosen modus operandi. If a dangerous predator were at the scene—mountain lions and grizzly bears both roamed where I worked—I could always return later to assess the calf's disposition. No need to steal somebody's lunch at the risk of triggering an attack. The pepper spray was my sidekick, a deterrent to repel an aggressor that I accidentally provoked. At the start of each year's field season, I trained my technicians and volunteers to use it.

On the other hand, I intended to recover as many useful tissues and as quickly as possible. Samples of heart, kidneys, lungs, liver, lymph nodes, and other internal organs could be cultured at the Wyoming State Veterinary Lab by my collaborator, Dr. Beth Williams, to diagnose predisposing conditions or diseases that compromised calves. When a complete carcass was found, the task was simple: pack the carcass out, freeze it whole, and ship it to the vet lab in Laramie, four hundred miles away, for a thorough examination. When the calf was partially consumed—the result of either predation or scavenging—I'd perform a field necropsy, the animal equivalent of a coroner's autopsy. I'd investigate if a calf had been killed and fed on by its assailant. Or had it died of disease or accident and then been discovered and scavenged by a carnivore? In either case, I'd plop sections of tissues into formalin for later histological examination and a duplicate set into plastic bags for culture of disease pathogens by the vet lab's diagnosticians.

These tissue treasures could solve the mystery of whether a calf's survival was compromised. A healthy calf may not fall prey to a coyote. One suffering from malnutrition, disease, or injury, however, might be slower, weaker, or less vigilant, providing the song dog a reprieve from stalking merely bite-sized meadow voles. Too easy it would be to blame the cunning and predatory prowess of a bear, coyote, or eagle feeding on a dead calf as the cause of its demise when, in fact, the victim may already have been at death's doorstep. In short, each mortality was a wildlife CSI episode.

Back in Timbered Island, as deep-ochre eyes glowered across this bruin's rusty-brown muzzle, I stood still as a fence post, my eyes unable to blink. As he tested the air with flaring nostrils, his jaws parted, exposing one-inch-long canines. With my only defense a flimsy aluminum antenna clutched in my left hand and the receiver box pressed against my gut, I felt a bit over-matched. If he chose to press the issue, parrying him with the antenna struck me as comic relief rather than a fair fight. A contest with a predictable outcome.

I estimated him at 250 pounds, a good-sized black bear for Jackson Hole, probably a boar. A good guess also because no cubs or yearlings hovered nearby. Across the narrow distance that separated us, I saw and heard a scapula crunch as he returned to the meal. *Okay, now what?*

Black bears are supposed to run away. Be afraid of humans. This one didn't get the memo, I guess. Of course, there are cases where black bears have attacked humans in North America. Unlike its larger cousin the grizzly, blacks seldom attack humans to protect a food source or to defend their cubs. Instead, investigations of black bear attacks conclude that these rare events are mostly acts of predation—a bear bizarrely intent on eating its victim. Knowing that ill-fated confrontations of black bears dining on people were highly unusual was somehow not reassuring.

I had two choices: retreat and return after the bear was full or chase him off the kill. A fifty-plus-pound calf—which this ten-day-old was likely to weigh—was more than one meal for a bear, even one of his size. He may well bed down nearby until his appetite returned, maybe hang around the area for another day or two. Soon, little of value would be left for me to collect for scientific inquiry. Secondary bacterial growth would compromise the usefulness of any remaining tissues, potentially overgrowing any disease-causing agent and degrading the diagnostic value of organ tissues. In a hushed voice, I radioed a welfare check to park dispatch: "Arrived at the site. Predator present."

At the sound of my voice, the bear shot me a paralyzing stare. I tried to avoid direct eye contact so as not to challenge him. Satisfied I was no threat, he returned to the elk veal, but he jerked his head up as I disconnected the receiver from the antenna and slowly placed it on the ground. I'd decided.

Later today I had to prepare equipment and arrange for tomorrow morning's 5:30 a.m. helicopter flight to capture another batch of calves. I couldn't return here until tomorrow afternoon. No, I would examine and recover the remaining entrails now, before they were tomorrow's bear poop. The bear had to go.

In my scariest bear imitation, I raised my arms, filled my lungs, and hoarsely wuffed several times and louder than I realized I could. Apparently startled by the odd-looking, bombastic ursine, the bear lumbered into the shadows of the forest.

Success! I gathered the telemetry gear and pressed forward to the calf's remains. The carcass was fresh. In classic bear fashion, the skin and peritoneal muscles along the belly had been split and peeled back. Some of the key organs—heart, lungs, and one kidney—were partially uneaten. Uncoagulated red blood, warm muscles, and the scarcity of flies all suggested the calf had been attacked and overcome by the bear. I'd learn more upon skinning and examining the neck and shoulders for killing wounds from canine punctures.

After retrieving the sampling equipment from my pack and beginning to scribble notes in the data sheet's blanks, I glanced up. The bear was back. Less than ten yards away, he was scenting and swaying his head from side to side. *Shit!* Angry bear imitation number two: Wuff! Wuff!! Wuuuff!!!

To my relief, he bolted away. But after several minutes, he returned again, seemingly sensing that he had nothing to fear and ready to reclaim his meal. *This was one persistent or hungry bear.*

Rather than try to finish the forensic work on-site, I bagged the carcass in plastic, lashed it to my pack, and began hotfooting it out of Timbered Island. Despite my best efforts to scare him off, the bear tagged after me for perhaps a hundred yards. He seemed intent on reclaiming his unfinished feast. Finally he lost interest as I neared the forest edge.

When I met with Ken, Al, and Billy later that day and regaled them with my Timbered Island adventure, all were disappointed that they weren't able to share in the fun. Fun? Maybe like watching someone else fall off a horse. More than once during the bear's pursuit of me, I thought about how handy it would be to blast him with a stream of bear repellant. If life's lessons are best learned from our mistakes, then this experience qualified as PhD credit.

But my coworkers got their chances to visit future mortality sites, some with bears and mountain lions present. And like me, from that day on, each was armed with a trusty can of pepper spray.

THIRTEEN

BABY ELK

Aerodynamically, the bumblebee shouldn't be able to fly; but the bumblebee doesn't know this, so it goes on flying anyway.

—Mary Kay Ash, *Heavenly Wisdom*

Hunched on a cramped bench seat, Billy and I peered from the acrylic bubble, with high anticipation. We were seeking the study's first victim.

Billy Helprin, a square-jawed, blond biologist, was one of my two seasonal assistants. I'd met Billy at the Teton Science School, north of Jackson, Wyoming, where he worked as an environmental educator. Now we sought to educate ourselves on the fine art of capturing newborn elk. The year before, I learned the basics. A colleague of mine, Francis Singer, had invited me to Yellowstone National Park to help with his own study of elk calf survival. On a glorious morning, we helicoptered across Gardner's Hole and the Lamar Valley, catching eight baby elk and fitting each with an expandable radio collar.

Now the job was all mine to engineer. Over the next three weeks—the last week of May through the fifteenth of June, when 80 percent of the year's calves would arrive—I needed to capture and mark fifty or more newborns.

From the airport near Jackson, we followed the Snake River north; then Jerry banked the Hiller UH-12E west along Cottonwood Creek. Like Billy and me, Jerry was new to this. Elk capture from helicopter was not on his long resume of piloting skills. We would all learn the fine points of this work together. Capturing elk calves would prove a consummate team endeavor.

Flying along Cottonwood Creek, we spotted a group of cows, female elk, ducking through a canopy of freshly erupted leaves. On the chopper's second circle, a calf darted into a clearing.

"There," exclaimed Billy. "Just now crossing the creek."

I remember anxiously anticipating this field research. Leading up to the first capture flight, I practiced grasping the first calf and rehearsing the handling procedures over and over in my mind. Now just ten minutes in the air and I had my initial opportunity. We landed on a terrace twice the height of the cottonwoods in the stream corridor below. Billy and I unplugged our helmets' avionics cords, piled out, and headed for the calf's last known location.

In retrospect, our first attempted capture was like a Laurel and Hardy episode. I was skeptical when the calf crossed Cottonwood Creek, swollen with snowmelt and churning with silt. Now I was certain. After pursuing the calf across the creek and then back again, I deduced this was no neonate but a rambunctious tyke a week or so old. Drenched to the crotch and laughing at our misadventure, we retreated up the bank to the helicopter. Once inside, two puddles of water began pooling on the chopper's floorboards. Jerry shook his head ever so slightly while pretending not to see.

Airborne again and not ten minutes later, we approached a forested terrace west of the Snake River. A lone cow stared back at us from the edge of a lime-leaved and ivory-trunked aspen grove. The forested terrace above her plunged to a sage-studded bench some two hundred feet below. She stood stock-still in a thicket of snowberry and sagebrush halfway down the slope. Should we be lucky enough to spot a calf in that undergrowth, we'd have to hike up from the lower terrace.

Elk seek solitude when they are ready to give birth, an antipredator strategy to avoid attracting unwanted attention. Lone females, I would come to learn, are often harbingers of a newborn nearby. On our second circle from two hundred feet above her, I spotted a flash of rich brown, conspicuously more rust-colored than the cow's shedding coat. On our next pass overhead, I confirmed the flash of color was a calf tucked in a snarl of snowberry thirty yards from its mother. The mother had unwittingly helped me. Twice she'd curled that graceful neck in her offspring's direction. Her sentinel instincts gave away the calf's direction. This was a behavioral cue I would obligingly exploit again and again with other devoted mothers.

Billy and I made mental notes of the calf's hideaway before Jerry set the Hiller down far beneath the elk. Grabbing the pack with its assortment of capture equipment, Billy followed as I weaved my way through the clutching sagebrush up the slope. When we reached the edge of the thicket, I whispered to Billy, "Circle around to where the calf was facing."

I wanted him to become its point of focus. As he shifted into position, I snuck to the opposite side of the calf. Hunching so low that my knees nearly bumped my chin with each step, I cautiously stalked closer.

I was but fifteen feet away when I finally glimpsed a shred of rust brown through the brush. With several quick steps, I lunged, braced my fall with my hands, and pinned the calf beneath my chest. It gave a piercing squeal out of fright, as my arms encircled its body. From the edge of the forest above us, where she had nervously retreated, the mother responded with a sharp alarm bark and then another. I slipped one elastic band of the neoprene blindfold under the chin and one behind the calf's ears and hog-tied both hind legs and one front, rodeo style, in a wrap of Velcro strap.

Now Billy and I went deliberately through the protocol we'd rehearsed in dry runs. With calipers I measured the height of the middle pair of incisors (5.2 mm), the upper canines (barely through the gum), new hoof growth (9.2 mm), and the diameter and condition of the umbilicus (11.5 mm with a dry scab). From these measurements and the hard nature of the hooves and dew claws, I would later determine the calf was four days old.

Lifting the tail, I told Billy, "It's a one-holer, a male."

Of course a two would've been a female.

A fifty-two-pound calf such as this would be remarkably strong. The Velcro strap restrained his legs as a precaution, should he try to escape. Enveloped in darkness, the calf was surprisingly relaxed. But when I suspended him from a spring scale hooked through the strap, his kicking let us know he didn't appreciate being treated like a sack of potatoes. As soon as the scale's indicator needle stopped bouncing, Billy recorded the weight. I lowered him back to the ground where he went limp once again. The expandable radio collar I fitted around his neck would provide us an electronic link to his travels.

Billy had been all business, recording each announced detail on a form in a metal clipboard. Now we looked at each other, grinned widely, and chuckled. Two fellow admirers of nature's creation, we shared an ebullient joy distinct to this kind of work. After removing the Velcro strap and blindfold, we stepped away and inhaled the scene: the cottonwood-choked Snake River floodplain winding beyond the Hiller where Jerry stood watching us; the towering Tetons cloaked in winter's wardrobe with spring still buried below; and this precious addition to the Jackson elk herd, its flank heaving with life and the promise of romping in unknown meadows bursting with wildflowers. We simply felt privileged that we too would know that meadow when his mother led him there, if, that is, he escaped the perils awaiting every newborn elk.

♣

This was the first of 164 neonates (they averaged three days old) I would capture during three years of studying survival of Jackson Hole's elk. After grizzly bears began colonizing the valley and gray wolves were reintroduced to Yellowstone National Park in the mid-1990s, I captured another 154 calves in a follow-up, comparative study. Results of those studies were published in science journals and in the book *Where Elk Roam*.

More than just subjects of our research to improve the elk herd's conservation, each captured calf was a precious new life. And for a few short minutes, I was interrupting its arrival into the world. Each would have to overcome an assortment of potential challenges—predators, diseases, hunting, accidents, and even birth defects—that would winnow each year's calf crop until barely half saw their first birthday. I surely didn't want to add to that equation.

Although the cow-calf bond is tenacious in elk and mothers sometimes watched us handle their offspring from close range, I was anxious about causing abandonment of calves. So beyond precautionary handling protocols, I designed my research to monitor our effects. By radio locating and observing the calves from fixed-wing aircraft three times weekly, I was heartened to find none of our marked calves was abandoned.

♣

Details of capturing those elk remain with me today. Some triggered the naming of the animals we stalked and caught. You see, we identified the fifty-three calves we captured in 1990 only by chronological number, 1–53. "Don't personalize the animals you work with" was the deeply ingrained message I learned from college professors. Marked individuals were no more than part of a data set. Scientists were to remain detached from their subjects, even if they had soft brown eyes and wet noses like puppies.

But practicality intervened. Twice each day—early morning and ten to twelve hours later—seven days a week through July, my technicians and I monitored the radio signal of each elk that was on the air. We'd built four fixed radio-tracking stations surrounding the southern half of GTNP and adjacent Bridger-Teton National Forest where most calves were captured and could be monitored (at least until their mothers hiked some of them to distant summer pastures). Each station was a six-foot-by-six-foot plywood shack with a fiberglass roof. An eighteen-foot steel mast exited the fiberglass roof. The mast sported a pair of huge twelve-element antennae on top that boasted a potential receiving range of twenty miles. Inside, one of us rotated the mast while listening through headphones to the radio signal of each calf. Where the signal of calf number 1, for example, was loudest, a pointer attached to the mast indicated the signal's direction on a compass rosette. Simultaneously, we recorded signal azimuths at the other tracking stations.

Whoever had the laptop computer called the others by walkie-talkie for each calf's compass bearings. As the bearings were entered, the computer program displayed the intersecting azimuths. In real time and like magic, each calf's location and coordinates appeared on a blue LCD map.

Listening for most of two hours to electronic beeping was a tiring routine—particularly when signals were faint; faded in and out; or were masked by citizen-band conversations, including the local pizza delivery guy. Although we were eager to learn the whereabouts of each elk, our communications about number so-and-so held no special meaning. We needed something more tangible than ID numbers. So in 1991 we began naming each elk we captured.

Some were conferred the name of a nearby geographic landmark: Davis we captured on Davis Hill; Rosie, atop Rosie's Ridge; Mystic we found in the heart of the 1981 Mystic Isle burn; Island, for the island we had to reach by fording flood-swollen Cottonwood Creek; and Mardy we seized within view of conservationist Mardy Murie's house. Unique capture circumstances spawned names for others. Mossy we found nestled in a cushioning bed of moss. Tagalong followed us partway back to the helicopter. Tubbs was particularly hefty for a two-day-old. When we snatched Swan, two trumpeter swans honked overhead. Big Mama was the calf whose outsized mother threatened to stomp us silly.

For a time, we even named calves after ourselves or other people. But that soon ended. When we learned of her namesake's demise, for example, someone had to break the news to Kathy. Another lesson we learned was to never bestow a charmed name. Lucky, as fate would have it, was eaten a week later by a bear.

Some calves left a special impression. These are the stories of four.

🌲

Like the first calf we captured near Cottonwood Creek, most others were spotted from the Hiller helicopter. Across thousands of acres of wildlands, that proved the most efficient way of finding and capturing a representative sample of newborns. I captured a smaller number from horseback. Whenever I rode during calving season, I shouldered a daypack stuffed with radio collars and capture equipment. Whether I was off to investigate an elk whose radio collar beeped double fast (indicating its owner may be dead) or I was bound for some other task, I just might chance upon a newborn elk.

My favorite refuge horse was a tall, bay gelding with a feathery blaze and four white socks. I liked his temperament when hazing elk on the refuge and his eagerness to set a fast pace. His name was Budweiser, Bud for short. We made a good working team. If a coworker joined me, he or she would ride Mich (short for Michelob) or maybe Red (short for Red).

Toward the end of the 1992 calving season, I found a free afternoon. With my flight budget depleted and the helicopter returned to its stable in Greybull, Wyoming, I hoped to add another calf or two to our present sample of forty-eight. For statistical adequacy, my research plan called for fifty radioed calves per season. Besides, Bud looked as though he could use some work.

Across an undulating tract of monotypic sagebrush, we headed toward a solitary blemish of pines. As we approached the thatch of lodgepoles, a lone cow elk bolted out. I'd searched for calves with Bud before, and I sensed he took it as great sport. So with a minimum of reigning or footwork, he quickly started circling the two acres of forest. From beneath a clump of perimeter sagebrush, a calf dodged into the trees. For several minutes thereafter, we played a game of hide-and-seek, as Bud and I searched for its hiding place.

When we spied the calf lying still, I dismounted, dropped the reins, and pulled off a successful stalk. As I worked the calf and filled out the paperwork, Bud grazed toward where I knelt. Moments later he nudged my shoulder. As I rubbed his muzzle, my other hand stroked the calf, whom of course I named Bud.

♣

Kathy McFarland was a soft-spoken biologist fresh out of college when I hired her. She was a dedicated field technician who loved the outdoors and the varied experiences of our elk research. She filled Billy Helprin's position in 1991 and enjoyed the thrill of flying and catching calves.

On a crisp June morning, cruising over a sea of sagebrush, we spotted a calf in a nondescript hiding place. When we seized the three-day-old as easily as a rag doll, no special name came to mind. However, this was no ordinary elk.

After finishing weighing and radio-collaring him, I laid this thirty-nine-pound calf (a touch small for his age) beneath the thickly crowned bush where I'd found him hiding. When freed from their blindfolds and leg restraints, younger calves often remained bedded; older ones were more likely to flee to their mothers. This one did neither. He was just plain indignant. He promptly bounced to his feet, backed stiffly away, and then lowered his head and charged! By now I'd caught 102 calves and had never witnessed this behavior. I was sitting on the ground, gathering calipers and other equipment, when his head smacked into my shoulder. But once was not enough. Twice more he backed deliberately away and followed with a resolute head butt. When I pushed him back, he bucked and boxed his front hooves at me.

After that final attack, I'd had enough. I leapt to my feet and shooed him away. In disbelief, Kathy and I gawked at each other.

"Bucky," she said. "His name should be Bucky."

♣

Because my project was on a tight budget, efficiency was a constant concern. I recruited and trained volunteers to radio-track elk and sample vegetation, and I scrounged used equipment whenever I could. Helicopter charter was a major but necessary expense. Only by improving our capture rate (the number of calves caught per hour) could I reduce the annual expense of flight time. So I constantly challenged myself, and my flying companions, to ferret out calves more adeptly.

During the first week of their lives, elk calves were hiders. They remained bedded beneath sagebrush and willows or in deadfall where their motionless spotted coats were concealed from predators, including the kind with big rotary wings. I wanted to catch the youngest calves that we could find, because older calves already had survived those most vulnerable, first days.

"Older calves make biased samples," I told my assistants. "If you see a calf traveling with a herd, and especially one running, it's probably not of interest to me."

I was primarily looking for bedded calves and any edge to help spot them. Besides a supersized mug of coffee—a standard component of my flight gear on our dawn-to-late-morning capture missions—better sunglasses topped the list. Based on recommendations from clay shooters and an acquaintance of mine from a sporting-goods store, I bought a fancy pair of metal-rimmed Ray-Bans with spiffy lenses of photochromatic amber glass. They seemed just the ticket to penetrate early-morning glare and still highlight the flash of a calf's rusty coat. Eighty bucks offended my checkbook, but it was worth the price, I reckoned. I'd trim my helicopter costs if they worked as their proponents assured me they would.

The very next morning's flight covered a mosaic of overgrown sagebrush and aspen-covered landscape east of Grand Teton National Park. This was a prime elk calving area. Its amply thick cover concealed calves the way cloudy water hides fish from an osprey.

Alan Strassler was flying with me that day in 1991. Al was an affable Massachusetts transplant who'd worked extensively with elk, raptors, and other wildlife across the West. He and Billy were my field assistants in 1990, and the three of us had become good friends. Billy liked to describe Al as stocky; balding; and having a single, thick eyebrow. I liked Al's good humor, including his impersonations that ranged from Bill Murray in *Caddyshack* to the *Saturday Night Live* character Mr. Bill. But I especially valued the way Al questioned different aspects of our work. It made me think about how I might do things better.

This was Al's second year working for me, and spotting calves had become friendly competition. By 10:00 a.m. we'd collared five. I'd spotted each of them. Yes! The Ray-Bans were working.

Then we flew nearly forty minutes more, before Al spotted calf number six. On the ground, I motioned him to approach in the direction of the calf's field of view, as usual, while I crept up behind the calf. As I got close enough to make my final lunge, the calf jumped from his bed. Surprised by his strength, I clutched his hind legs as he drug me a few yards through the brush. After

I'd wrestled him to the ground and slipped the blindfold over his eyes, I heard Al laughing as he approached. Besides a nasty scratch across my forehead, twisted frames of my new Ray-Bans dangled from one ear. The calf's conquest that day made his christening a no-brainer. We agreed to call this one Ray Bans.

♣

All thirty-five hours of my capture flights in 1990 were with Jerry Ewen. The flying was technical with lots of hovering and slow circling, always at low elevations. Landings were wherever Jerry could squeeze the Hiller into the brush or gaps in forest patches. We developed a smooth working relationship, and I trusted his flying skills in this dicey work. I'd asked and expected Jerry back as my pilot the next year. However, another job and a scheduling conflict at Hawkins and Powers Aviation, where he worked, took him elsewhere. Instead, Paul was our pilot in 1991. A fortyish, tall, outgoing man, he presented quite the opposite demeanor to Jerry's methodical, low-key approach to the job. Seems I was forever prodding Paul, like a headstrong horse, to fly the searching pattern that I wanted and not whatever stoked his fire.

We were working the Central Valley of Grand Teton Park, and it had been a successful morning. So far we had captured nine calves, but we had flown far longer than usual—over six hours, including two refueling stops, since we'd lifted off at 6:10 a.m. One of us spotted a cow nursing a calf on a densely packed sagebrush bench. Between us the bench dropped abruptly to a flat far below. Beyond the pair, a group of maybe thirty more elk wove through a ragged fringe of aspen that faded into an opaque stand of lodgepole pine. Whether it was from flying fatigue or just wanting to cowboy-in a quick landing, Paul headed straight for them without circling to reconnoiter a landing site. He settled the Hiller into the sagebrush just twenty yards short of where the elk had been. Apparently signaling her calf to hide in place, the mother then fled to the tree line.

This we saw often. Instinctively responding to the alarm bark of cows, new calves dropped to the ground and froze in place. No more than the twitch of an ear or pulsing black nostrils to give their presence away. Meanwhile, their mothers may graze one hundred or more yards distant. I recall one calf I caught that appeared to be abandoned, until I watched its mother return to it from one-third mile away. This defense behavior serves them well for the first week or so of life, until they've grown big and robust enough to join the safety of herd life.

A mother returns and suckles her calf four to six times per day. During this hider stage when they expend little energy, I found female calves gained three pounds per day, and males put on three and a half pounds of weight daily. As additional precaution during these nursing bouts, the mother consumes the calf's urine and feces and licks the calf extensively to reduce such giveaway scent. This protective avoidance has proven a successful maternal behavior for elk and for other species of large mammals, such as deer and pronghorn antelope.

Catching and processing our eighty-second calf was routine. But that episode in elk quest quickly took a bad turn. A stiff midday breeze had arisen out of the south. The Hiller faced north. Upon lifting off, it would need to avoid a broadly branching aspen at twelve o'clock before turning windward to gain lift beneath its rotary wing. Unfortunately, it didn't work out that way.

As we rose from the ground, the right strut (the paired struts are the feet of the helicopter) tangled in a gnarly sagebrush bush. First it twisted us slightly and then rolled us forward. As Paul applied the cyclic control to lift the nose of the ship, we lurched forward and plopped down, bounced, and came to a halt. From the outbound positions on the bench seat, Al and I looked wide-eyed at each other and then at Paul, who was sputtering expletives between us.

"What happened?" I blurted.

"Sonofabitch, we just had a tail rotor strike!" came Paul's reply.

After he shut down the engine and we all bailed out, he pointed to a dent in the leading edge of one of the two tail rotor blades. Some more words followed from Paul that weren't exactly, "Jeez, that's too bad." Brusquely he returned to the cockpit and informed park dispatch by radio that we'd be on the ground for a short while, a standard procedure each time we landed to capture a calf. No mention of the accident.

Our crash landing happened so fast that neither Al nor I had time to panic or anything else. When we compared notes later, we both knew that when the ship had rolled forward, the top rotor blades came close to walloping the ground. Had that happened, the acrylic bubble would be battered as it cartwheeled across the sagebrush. Inside, we'd be thrashed like clothes in a dryer.

After Paul pointed out the tail rotor damage, Al and I huddled. We agreed we were going nowhere else in the Hiller that day. We knew the park's Central Valley well enough to estimate that the inside-park road was about three miles away. But a two-track spur passed just half that distance to the south. *A walk in the park to us!*

I raised Kathy on my portable radio. "Can you give us a lift?" I asked and described where to meet us.

Satisfied in his mind that the Hiller was good to go, Paul ordered us to load up. "I'm going to fire the engine to see how the tail rotor performs."

"I think we'll just walk to the road," I said and suggested he might want to join us. Some back-and-forth followed about the prudent means of traveling home. But Paul was determined to fly the eighteen miles back to the Jackson airport. With our decisions made, the three of us cleared the brush from the helicopter's struts.

As Paul revved the Hiller's engine, Al and I shot anxious looks at each other and moved well out of the way. With only him on board, he'd easily get the Hiller airborne and turned south—if the tail rotor held together. As the ship shuddered and rose, I couldn't stop wondering, *Why trust this wounded bird with your life?*

Al and I didn't start hiking until the chopper was airborne, then southbound, and finally beyond the horizon. Like an impending train wreck from which you can't look away, we watched until it had faded from sight. We both knew the tail rotor could disintegrate, sending the ship gyrating earthbound. But it didn't. No telltale explosions reached our ears. No fireballs burst into the sky. Following a disparaging critique as we hiked to the road, Al and I agreed that Paul must live a charmed life.

The Hiller landed safely at the airport. And later that day a company mechanic flew in and replaced the tail rotor. I can only image the tongue-lashing Paul received for risking a pricey flying ship, and his own life, without first consulting the boss. And if we'd chosen to chance it, two more lives would have hung in the balance. It was one of those decisions that I've looked back on and felt that discretion was indeed the better part of valor.

Kathy was waiting for us at the gravel road. When we told her the story of our last calf capture and the helicopter close call, she just shook her head in disbelief.

"Hey, I've got a good name for this calf," Al said. "I think we should call him Crash."

Two days later, we were back flying but, at my insistence, with a new pilot.

Not surprisingly, I learned that Paul was no longer working for Hawkins and Powers by summer's end. Recklessness of another brand caught up with him. He'd taken liberties with a company Jet Ranger in Oregon, using it for trysts with a girlfriend. Company owner Dan Hawkins wasn't amused. Paul's idea of wildlife work had gone too far for the boss.

FOURTEEN

THE CIRCLE

The frog does not drink up the pond in which he lives.
—Sioux proverb

It's a universal truth that much of what we see around us follows a circle. Considered the father of modern observational astronomy, Galileo had it right: our planet does not hover motionless at the center of the universe; it orbits the sun. Chris Columbus didn't fall off the edge of the earth when he set sail from Spain seeking a new trade route to the East Indies. Whether it be moon phases, tidal patterns, or the annual changing of the seasons, recurrence is the norm. Examples are endless. No clearer is this principle than in nature's rhythm of renewal and continuance—the water and nitrogen cycles; the ten-year cycle of snowshoe hare abundance; and life's circle of birth, death, decomposition, and rebirth.

Native American cultures and, for that matter, aboriginal peoples around the globe display a keen understanding of the circle of life and its importance to their own. Seasons for gathering fruits and tubers and setting nets for migrating fish and using fire to regularly rejuvenate plant life to facilitate their hunting of game—these and many other recurring activities bound the people to the land, gave rise to their customs, and fashioned their lifestyles.

This raises a second truth about the natural world: all things are interconnected. The trophic linkages that provide community stability among herbivores, predators, scavengers, and detritivores are complex relationships shaped by natural selection. Without our help in the slightest, these processes endure like a metronome. Naturalist John Muir phrased it this way: "When one tugs at a single thing in nature, one finds it attached to the rest of the world."

In our technocratic world, modern *Homo sapiens* may dwell less on these things than our ancestors who lived closer to the land. Manipulation of nature for our convenience is a hallmark of our domination of the "untamed" natural world. This idea of untamed nature struck Native peoples as peculiar. Oglala Sioux chief Luther Standing Bear noted, "Only to the white man was nature a 'wilderness' and only to him was the land 'infested' with 'wild' animals and 'savage' people. To us it was tame."

Contemporary society's efforts to control things, or to direct natural processes toward desired ends, often spawn unintended consequences. I gained some experience with that during my career as the National Elk Refuge biologist, managing the public's wildlife and coordinating the winter feeding of thousands of elk. Historically, wildlife management favored species that people held dear over less worthy species. Only decades ago, that meant eradicating predators (the bad animals, such as coyotes and cougars and wolves and wolverines) in order for the good animals, like deer and game birds, to prosper. Over time, we've changed our thinking about this, and ever so slowly our behavior.

Indeed, when we think we know better, we're often humbled to find that our anthropocentric tinkering serves only to disrupt nature's fine-tuning. The authority of these truths—the circularity and interconnectedness of nature—is distilled in the following example where my own intervention boomeranged.

♠

I was no less anxious than the elk for each spring's arrival. As the feed trucks made their last runs in late March or early April, I breathed a sigh of relief. No major disease outbreak had befallen the elk—an omnipresent cloud of concern that followed refuge managers like a shadow.

As the high arc of the sun passed north of the equator, its intensified energy transformed the land. Snowmelt wells ringed warmed rocks, tufts of grass, and brush. Outward spread the thaw, like ripples from a rising trout. Soon brown rivulets shredded the refuge's white blanket. Elk roamed widely, seeking the awakening delicacies sprouting from south-facing ditch banks and knobs. Feed trucks drew fewer and fewer customers. Then, almost overnight, a sheen of emerald stirred Poverty Flats' tawny plain to life, and wildflowers began to cheer lifeless hills.

The return of migratory birds dazzled me with flight and song. Bluebirds flashed from rock to post; blackbirds and wrens filled Flat Creek's marsh. Great blue herons again fished stoically in oxbows. Canada geese tucked the miracle of eggs beneath their breasts. Overhead, the primeval chorus of sandhill cranes announced spring was soon to come.

Each year, one pair of geese laid its eggs among grass and wildflowers on the sod roof of the refuge's visitor center. One by one, at their parents' urging, the dusky hatchlings leapt into the void. They fluttered earthbound like oversized snowflakes. They plopped onto water and were promptly swimming, as though each egg had contained an Olympic training pool.

Visitors asked why this pair chose the rooftop corner of a bustling building. Why not, like more sensible geese, pick an earthbound nest site? Why a fifteen-foot high dive for their hatchlings' first swim, rather than a waddle to nearby water? The refuge's healthy population of coyotes, skunks, and mink were the likely answer. All were fond of eggs, and a goose's clutch of eight to twelve affords a fine feast. But skunks and mink were no more plentiful on the NER than most other places. Coyotes, well that's another story.

Once the elk migrated to summer pastures, coyotes' feasting on five-hundred-pound carcasses of diseased and old-aged animals quickly ended. They were back to full-time mousing, hunting Uinta ground squirrels emerging from winter dens, and eating whatever else these opportunists could find. As it turns out, they were quite good at searching out nests of waterfowl and probably other ground-nesting birds. It seemed that geese were in a perpetual race of wits with terrestrial predators, especially coyotes, to protect their nests. Every island in refuge ponds and Flat Creek's meanders was a coveted nesting site. But encircling moats proved no match for at least one wily coyote.

National Elk's public-use specialist, Jim Griffin, was a keen observer of refuge residents. As Jim drove to the refuge maintenance shop one April morning, he spied a robbery in progress. Through binoculars, he watched the crime unfold.

On the tip of an oblong island, a pair of geese had successfully nested for several years. A lone coyote paced the pond's shoreline. Could this be the day the pair's luck ran out? The coyote peered longingly at the hunkered, nesting goose; fidgeted; and tested the water with a paw. Suddenly, he plunged in and paddled to the island. Despite the defensive goose's battering wings, the coyote mouthed an egg, swam back to the mainland, laid down the egg, dug a shallow hole, and placed the egg inside. One by one, Jim watched the coyote make ten such trips. Then the thief covered the eggs and left without pausing to sample his plunder—a hollow victory for two distraught empty nesters.

Jim's story only added to my concern about the low hatching success of refuge geese. I proposed a project to the Jackson High School's shop teacher. With a design I provided, his students fashioned eight wire nesting baskets. We fastened the baskets atop steel posts anchored in ponds and Flat Creek's marsh and packed them with hay for nesting.

The next spring, every basket was occupied by a pair of geese. Each pair hatched a brood of goslings. This continued for several years as a new problem arose. The refuge was producing too many geese. Tourists complained about the slick of goose poop on the nearby town park's grounds—now a grand grazing lawn for geese. Indeed, you could barely step anywhere without landing in goose grease. Flip-flops and bare feet were out of the question. The geese were now winning the war of wits, and I had another life's lesson reinforced.

Whenever we tweak nature to our preference or pleasure, there follow reactions or consequences we may not anticipate. I called a halt to replenishing nesting hay in the baskets (each winter elk skated across the ponds and emptied each one). The local goose population leveled off. More tourists picnicked in the park. Refuge coyotes appeared especially pleased.

♣

My tinkering with Canada goose production is symbolic of the National Elk Refuge's most celebrated, scrutinized, and controversial program. Ask someone who's even vaguely familiar, "What does the refuge do?" You will likely hear, "That's where they feed the elk."

From December to April, the largest concentration of elk in the world assembles there each year. Like a miniature Serengeti, hosts of antlered, tawny animals, right next to a full-service tourist town, make Jackson a unique destination among Rocky Mountain recreational resorts. But the spectacle of so many magnificent creatures, beneath a backdrop of Grand Teton National Park's soaring Teton Range, isn't wholly a product of Wyoming being so lightly populated by people and its absence of farmsteads, subdivisions, and shopping malls. In fact, not all that long ago, most of the elk from what is now called the Jackson elk herd roamed much farther to seek winter pastures. Rather than tough out the snows of Jackson Hole (it's no accident the valley boasts two premier ski areas, dogsled races, and the World Championship Snowmobile Hill Climb), most of the elk migrated 150–200 miles to Southwest Wyoming's desert country. Winter winds there sweep ribbons of grasslands free of snow. It's a modest trip for elk, which can cover ten, fifteen, or more miles daily during migration. But as is increasingly the fate of animal migrations around the globe, it ended. During the late 1800s, the migrants were steadily killed off to feed the transcontinental railroad crews and supply food to mining camps. Others were killed by market hunters, who sold the meat and hides in eastern markets, and by homesteaders, ranchers, recreational hunters, and the U.S. Cavalry. By 1917 the fall spectacle of thousands of elk coursing southward from the mountains surrounding Jackson Hole was over.

The carnage predated the regulation of hunting, and the level of exploitation was unsustainable. Nearly all wild large mammals were on the verge of vanishing from North America by 1900. From a continental population estimated at 10 million elk, only fifty thousand remained by the early twentieth century. Many of those were in the Yellowstone–Jackson Hole region, a wild landscape now called the Greater Yellowstone Area. At the same time, state and federal officials began provisioning hay to the elk in the Jackson Valley.

At the outset, winter feeding was a noble effort to rescue a species but also served to keep the animals from raiding ranchers' haystacks (grass harvested from the valley bottoms to feed livestock). With protective measures, a large wintering herd built up in Jackson Hole, helping fuel a nascent tourist economy. Most elk wintered at the present site of the National Elk Refuge, which was established in 1911. Winter feeding reduced winter mortality—which normally pares down big game herds during periodic severe winters—boosting numbers beyond what the wildland grazing could support. As numbers swelled, so did the feeding program and the surplus of elk that needed to be removed each year.

Hunters flocked to the valley each fall, from all across the nation. The state of Wyoming, which sets population goals and issues commensurate numbers of hunting licenses, established a target population size to satisfy the recreational demand and to enhance the growing tourist economy. A large elk herd produced a large surplus for hunters, which meant more income for Wyoming from the sale of licenses.

So many elk had to be removed from the herd annually that in 1950 a federal law established an elk reduction program in Grand Teton National Park—the only national park in the lower forty-eight states with a big game hunting program. Another unintended consequence of the supersized elk-herd policy is that a grizzly bear, a federally recognized threatened species, was killed by an elk hunter in Grand Teton National Park in 2012. In response to this incident, which investigators concluded was justifiable self-defense, federal authorities predicted that four more grizzly bears are likely to be killed in the park through 2022 in connection with elk hunting, as will two more bears in the National Elk Refuge (yes, elk are also hunted on the same refuge where they are fed). Furthermore, those bear deaths will be exempt from liability under the Endangered Species Act. Without the refuge feeding program, a smaller elk herd may not require a hunting program in one or both of those national sanctuaries.

Like the riddle of the chicken and the egg, a large elk harvest and an artificially bloated herd were dependent on each other and became institutionalized as a part of western Wyoming culture. "How many elk?" you must be wondering. And at what cost to feed them? Over the past century, an average of 7,400 elk per year were fed at an annual cost of $500,000–$750,000, in today's dollars. Feeding the herd is an expensive proposition, and Wyoming pays for only half the hay. The American taxpayers finance the remainder and the associated costs of feeding the animals.

Of course, elk are perfectly capable of fending for themselves when their numbers are in balance with their habitat. They have done so throughout the western mountains of North America for more than ten thousand years. Winter feeding, a practice we associate with livestock production, is anomalous wildlife management. So unusual, in fact, that of the estimated 1 million elk now roaming North America, just 3 percent are fed in winter by government agencies. Three-fourths of those inhabit western Wyoming.

So at the core of the Greater Yellowstone Area—the largest wild ecosystem in the lower forty-eight states (some 18 million acres)—is this program of propagating elk. It's a program propelled by human self-interest and supportive government policies, rather than by what may be best for the wildlife or the ecosystem as a whole. Without reestablishing those ancient migrations to Wyoming's desert, could the landscape support a vigorous herd if feeding were ended? Of course.

Of the lands that the Jackson elk roam, 97 percent are in public ownership: national parks and forests and refuges plus state-administered lands. The feeding program draws most of the elk to a fraction of the area. They're habituated—addicted to the siren song of easy pickings dispensed from feed wagons. Without the hay handouts, instead of the eleven thousand head the state prescribes (and a population size exceeded most years), the herd would likely number half as many—still a large number of elk.

Seldom has the consequential question been candidly debated: just because we *can* produce an outsized herd by feeding hay to wild elk, *should* we? Indeed, these are wild elk, and the fundamental trait that distinguishes wild animals from our livestock and pets is wildlife's *independence* from us. All they require is suitable habitat and room to roam.

♣

Feedgrounds are fixtures in Wyoming, like the state's bucking-bronco license plate, Devil's Tower, and horizontal snowstorms in December. In addition to the National Elk Refuge, the state of Wyoming feeds thousands more elk at twenty-two additional locations. While feeding has produced short-term recreational and economic benefits and curbed conflicts and competition between elk and livestock, it does so at significant long-term economic and ecological costs.

Jackson's elk don't exist in a vacuum. They are part of a diverse web of species—plants and animals with which they share the land. I became convinced during my tenure as refuge biologist—and so have many other conservationists—that winter feeding was a practice that had long outlived its necessity and usefulness. Combined with common sense, the accumulated research findings on the subject made that clear.

Overstocking the range with too many animals has damaged the very habitat that refuge managers are charged with stewarding. Not only do degraded shrublands and woodlands do the elk no favors, but other species of wildlife have suffered as a consequence. Maybe the most egregious outcome of crowding the elk each winter is a population plagued by diseases—chronic ailments that rarely reach similar prevalences in herds that are not fed. Despite being provided daily rations of nutritious alfalfa for two to three months each winter, the Jackson elk are arguably the most diseased and unhealthy elk herd on the continent, predisposed, like warehoused poultry and feedlot livestock, to the vicissitudes of overpopulation. The feedgrounds are recycling centers for scabies (loss of hair from parasitic infestations), hemorrhagic septicemia (a sometimes-fatal bacterial illness), foot rot (a debilitating hoof infection), bovine brucellosis (a disease elk contracted from cattle that causes females to abort), and other maladies. Fortunately, none of these extant, infectious diseases pose a significant threat to the elk herd's viability. But the future is not so certain.

Chronic wasting disease—a neurodegenerative disease of elk, deer, and moose—is moving relentlessly across Wyoming toward elk feedgrounds. Unlike the diseases listed in the preceding paragraph, chronic wasting disease is an infectious disease against which elk have no immune defense. It's 100 percent fatal. In the book *Where Elk Roam*, I wrote that "feedgrounds could become de facto biological 'Superfund' sites contaminated with infectious prions (the disease-causing agent of chronic wasting disease) proven highly resistant to environmental and chemical degradation." Winter after winter, as elk are drawn to the feedgrounds for easy living, the level of soil contamination will increase. And chronic wasting disease is unlikely to be the last emerging threat to elk crowded like kids in a daycare center where contagious bugs readily spread from one child to the next. But unlike a coughing and feverish child who's kept home from school, sick elk can't be kept from mingling with the herd.

Any prospects for change in Wyoming's elk paradigm have remained slim, though not for lack of trying by conservationists and a failed legal challenge or two. But as of 1997 the landscape began to shift. Believe it or not, occasionally wise policy making in Washington DC can nudge the levers of reform and make the wheels stop spinning, as we shall see in this book's next chapter.

Like my brief foray into goosing goose production, elk management in Jackson Hole is myopic. Shaped by political and economic interests, the directed outcome runs contrary to conservation of a balanced natural order. By contrast, unfettered wild nature serves no master. It answers only to the weather and the organically orchestrated interaction and struggle among all creatures.

Humankind has not woven the web of life.
We are but one thread within it.
Whatever we do to the web, we do to ourselves.
All things are bound together.
All things connect.

Chief Seattle, Suquamish Indian Tribe, 1854

The web is the great circle.

FIFTEEN

EMPTY FORESTS

It is that range of biodiversity that we must care for—
the whole thing—rather than just one or two stars.
—David Attenborough, BBC interview

On August 3, 2011, a federal court of appeals ruled on a case that challenged winter feeding of elk and bison on the National Elk Refuge. For the first time, a court decision asserted that the refuge's winter feeding program was contrary to the refuge's mission and legal mandates under the National Wildlife Refuge System Improvement Act of 1997. That legislation provides guidance for management of the 560 national wildlife refuges that span more than 150 million acres across all fifty states. The three-judge panel admonished the U.S. Fish and Wildlife Service, which administers the refuge system: "The whole point of a National Elk *Refuge* is to provide a sanctuary in which populations of healthy, reproducing elk can be sustained. The Refuge can hardly provide such a sanctuary if, every winter, elk and bison are drawn by the siren song of human-provided food to what becomes, through the act of gathering, a miasmic zone of life-threatening diseases." However, the court stopped short of specifying a date when winter feeding must end.

What calls into question the gathering and feeding of animals is that the Improvement Act charges all refuges "to ensure that the biological integrity, diversity, and environmental health of the [Refuge] System are maintained." This requirement pertains to both the animals and the habitats that sustain them on refuges. In the case of the National Elk Refuge, not only is the health of the elk themselves compromised by diseases such as brucellosis, hemorrhagic septicemia, foot rot, and scabies (and the looming threat of chronic wasting disease, a 100 percent fatal neurodegenerative disease advancing toward western Wyoming), but refuge shrublands and woodlands have been overbrowsed by far too many elk. The feeding program, by definition, is confirmation that the range has been overstocked. Were populations limited to what their food sources could sustain without harm, feeding elk and bison would be unnecessary.

One might ask, "How is there overbrowsing when the animals are fed?" Feeding occurs an average of seventy days of the six months elk and bison spend on the refuge each year. Even during the feeding season, the animals continue to balance their diets with a diversity of grasses, shrubs, and other plants they forage. As a consequence of chronic browsing, 95 percent of tall willows have disappeared from refuge lands; cottonwood shoots have no chance of becoming trees; and half of all 143 aspen stands on the refuge are deteriorating, unable to replace dying mature stems with new saplings.

The upshot is not only a visually changed landscape but a declining abundance of other vertebrate species, especially birds. Investigations by refuge biologists, other scientists, and graduate students have documented this erosion of biodiversity. Flat Creek too—an important spawning stream for Snake River cutthroat trout that courses through the refuge—lacks the streamside cover to moderate water temperatures and limit siltation. While the absence of willows may make fly casting easier, hydrologist Alan Galbraith also found that it makes for less stable stream banks, less terrestrial insect life to nourish fish, and less screening of fish from avian predators.

The red-tailed hawk provides an example of how subtle changes in habitat insidiously reduce densities of animals. In the 1940s and 1950s, Frank and John Craighead first catalogued nesting pairs in the Jackson Valley. John's son Derek and colleagues have repeated those original surveys and have identified a number of natural and anthropogenic changes related to waning redtail numbers.

When I arrived at the refuge in 1982, a pair of redtails nested in a small aspen stand near the refuge's McBride feedground. Like other groves near elk feedgrounds, this stand grew few new stems, and only two dozen live trees remained in the overstory. In May 1993 graduate student Roger Smith and I banded the two nestlings hatched by that pair. Not only was the nest tree no longer living; it was the last stem standing in the grove. At least the redtails had picked the right tree for their nest!

That final aspen soon joined its fallen cohorts, and the redtails were forced to find a new nest tree. Like most bird species, redtails are territorial, so the pair's greater challenge was to establish a territory uncontested by other pairs. Derek Craighead notes that red-tailed hawk territories—and even specific nest trees—are rigidly occupied for decades in Jackson Hole, and a finite number of suitable spaces occur on the land. Birds, like aspen, disappear one pair or grove at a time.

All species in a habitat or ecosystem are interdependent, from lowly bacteria to top-rung predator. None is dispensable, though some are certainly valued more than others by humans. No more eloquently has this concept been stated than in Aldo Leopold's *A Sand County Almanac.* "The outstanding discovery of the twentieth century is not radio or television, but rather the complexity of the land organism. . . . If the land mechanism as a whole is good, then every part is good, whether we understand it or not. If the biota, in the course of eons, has built something we like but do not understand, then who but a fool would discard seemingly useless parts? To keep every cog and wheel is the first precaution of intelligent tinkering."

During the past 550 million years, the planet's biodiversity has suffered five major collapses. Those mass extinctions resulted from increased volcanism, sea-level flux associated with climate change, or major asteroid impacts. A sixth mass extinction is now underway. Pick a continent, sea, or ecosystem, the effects of pollution, deforestation, desertification, urban sprawl, invasive species, excessive exploitation of species for food and trade, and global climate change have conspired to accelerate the background species extinction rate by an estimated one hundredfold to one thousandfold.

Because life and the threats to it are not spread evenly across the planet, some places like the Greater Yellowstone Area—with much of its 18 million acres federally protected in national parks, forests, and refuges—are more secure than other ecosystems. It is in the tropical and subtropical regions and certain temperate forests where biodiversity is richest and species losses are out of control. Tropical rain forests, for example, cover just 3 percent of the earth's surface but support over half of all known species of plants and animals.

In a seminal 1988 paper in the *Environmentalist*, Norman Meyers identified ten tropical forest hotspots characterized both by exceptional levels of plant endemism (found nowhere else in the world) and by serious levels of habitat loss. The concept of biological hotspots has been widely adopted to focus conservation strategies toward those areas where biodiversity is at greatest risk. Subsequent reassessments have added twenty-four more hot spots, due to rampant fragmentation and destruction of natural plant communities.

Conservation International estimates that the thirty-four hotspots have lost a combined 86 percent of their original habitat and now cover only 2.3 percent of the earth's surface. Yet they contain more than half the world's plant species and an astounding 43 percent of terrestrial vertebrate species. In biological hot spots like the Guinean Forests of West Africa and the Tropical Andes of South America, catalogued species pale by comparison with scientists' estimates of those still undiscovered. Untold numbers face extinction before they ever become known to science.

Off the eastern coast of Africa, one such biological hot spot is the island of Madagascar. Madagascar's long isolation from neighboring continents (it is the oldest island in the world, isolated for at least 65 million years) has produced a unique mix of plants and animals. Slash-and-burn agriculture has replaced 90 percent of Madagascar's natural plant communities with plantations and livestock pasture—largely during the past century. Adaptation and evolution of animal species cannot keep pace with such rapid changes, resulting in ongoing and irretrievable losses of native life-forms. The great tragedy is that 90 percent of the island's animal species are endemic. When they're gone from Madagascar, they're extinct on planet earth.

In October 2007 I spent three weeks 750 miles to the west of Madagascar in KwaZulu-Natal province of South Africa. Conservation International labels this area along the eastern coast of Southern Africa the Maputaland-Pondoland-Albany Hotspot. About 80 percent of South Africa's remaining forests grow here. These warm temperate forests are home to the highest tree diversity of any temperate forests in the world, nearly six hundred tree species.

After a week exploring the relatively pristine Drakensberg Mountains, my wife, Diana, and I drove east. Beginning some sixty miles inland of the Indian Ocean, the rolling landscape of grasslands dotted with poor rural villages, farm plots, and goat herds drastically changed. Amid steeper terrain and a moister climate, the land morphed to a monoculture of tree plantations.

From any of the ridges that Highway R34 topped, a sea of eucalyptus in various stages of rotational harvest sprawled in every direction. Occasional signs reading "Mondi: Forestry for Life" identified the corporate landlord. Mondi is an international paper and packaging company operating in thirty-four countries. Mondi Business Paper's South African holdings include over 1.2 million acres of forestry plantations, making this one of the largest plantation units in the world. A paper mill in Merebank and woodchip mill, pulp mill, and corrugated case machinery in Richards Bay complete its South African interests.

I learned from Mondi's website that global production of paper in 2008 accounted for about 2.5 percent of the world's industrial production, totaling approximately 338 million metric tons. Global demand for printing and writing paper is rising 4.6 percent per year. In that lucrative arena, Mondi's a rapidly growing player producing remarkable returns for shareholders. The forest-products industry has received media attention concerning alleged unethical forest-management practices and wood sourcing.

Given its stated commitment to reduce energy consumption and emissions of carbon dioxide and other toxic byproducts and to work with local communities, I suspect Mondi is better than most at addressing its environmental impacts. The company's website emphasizes its efforts to achieve sustainable development, "by demonstrating active stewardship of land, water and biodiversity." Yet the reforesting of miles and miles of Africa's coastal forests with monocultures of nonnative trees belies the marketing. The effects on endemic species must be considerable. I decided to investigate.

I steered our rented Toyota Corolla onto the roadside next to one of the "old-growth" stands. Walking between evenly spaced rows of evenly planted trees—spacings calculated to maximize growth and production of wood fiber—I found debris from the tree canopies and little else on the forest floor. For lack of life, the eucalyptus may as well have been giant fence posts. No singing birds on this spring day; no signs of mammals.

On an adjacent, recently harvested tract, acres of evenly spaced stumps studded reddish-brown topsoil churned by logging equipment. Slash scattered in the course of felling trees provided the only cover for mouse, mongoose, or lark. A four-foot palm, having somehow escaped the jaws of cultivation and logging machinery, provided an anomalous, almost-comic contrast to the stark landscape. Yet its measly shelter offered no refuge for vervet monkey, sunbird, or snake.

This Australian import to fertile KwaZulu-Natal may bedevil the land long after we find a paper substitute or depart ourselves. The aromatic eucalyptus oils that we use to make cough medicine and to disinfect household surfaces kill germs because in larger doses they're toxins designed to ward off competitive plants. Few insects tolerate eucalyptus; and with little to eat, few birds forage or nest among them. That was evident to my eyes and ears.

Later that day, we visited nearby Dlinza Forest Nature Reserve, adjacent to the bustling town of Eschowe. What a sensory contrast! This six-hundred-acre tract is one of several relic forests protected in the province. So little light filters through the triple-canopy forest that only the most shade-tolerant shrubs, ferns, vines, and fungi grace the forest floor. Elephants no longer trumpet here. Like Yellowstone Park's elk and grizzlies, they need room to roam. But the forest remains rich in smaller biota, including the Dlinza Forest pinwheel snail, a species recorded nowhere else in the world. In this island oasis, sixty-five endemic bird and eighty butterfly species have been counted to date.

Along an aerial boardwalk, we ascended from the forest floor to the upper canopy, sixty-five feet above. At each level, another biota revealed itself. At the lowest, red duikers browse leaves of the forest num-num shrub; skipper butterflies deposit their eggs on the moth-fruit; and the endangered spotted thrush secrets among the white violet bush and dragon tree. At midcanopy, yellow-eyed canaries flit among epiphytic orchids and ferns that cling to strangler fig and giant umzimbeet trees. Pied barbets, emerald cuckoos, trumpeter hornbills, green twinspots, and golden-tailed woodpeckers dine on fruits and insects among tangles of branches.

The boardwalk culminates in a steel-latticed tower that bursts from the humid greenery. It offers a magnificent view of the arboreal canopy from above. A lesser double-collared sunbird hovers at arm's length, drawing nectar from tubular pink flowers. The ecological equivalent of North American hummingbirds, the sunbird is part of yet another fauna—including the paradise flycatcher, grey cuckooshrike, and powerful crowned eagle—that finds plant and animal prey in the uppermost forest.

It's a powerful experience, gazing across the undulating shades of olive, jade, and emerald. If a place can smell green, this is it. Yellow swallowtails flutter by; black-faced vervet monkeys scamper from limb to limb; and the rising, otherworldly crescendo of the purple-crested lourie booms from a perch veiled by limbs and leaves. The sensory overload is intoxicatingly surreal. We spend far longer than planned to drink it all in.

As nightfall envelops the forest, a whole new fauna of tree frogs and rodents, bats and bushbabies, large-spotted genets and wood owls comes to life. I don't know the total number of species inhabiting Dlinza. No one really does. The host of invertebrates and microbes hidden within bark, soil, and litter alone would be staggering. But just among vertebrates, the disparity between Dlinza and a Mondi tree plantation must equal several orders of magnitude.

🌲

Whether a Jackson Hole aspen grove or a Madagascar rain forest, when a natural habitat is degraded or supplanted, more than endemic vegetation is lost. The nesting red-tailed hawk may not find a suitable territory elsewhere. Indri lemurs cannot migrate across a slash-and-burn landscape to another suitable patch of shrinking forest. Absent the forest's green umbrella, soils parch and nutrients wash away. As the trees perish, so do associated life-forms. A woodland or forest is more than just trees.

This was the scientists' message during the 1990s debate pitting old-growth-forest logging against conservation of the Pacific Northwest's northern spotted owls. It's not strictly about the owl but about the community of life that shares the owl's home. This commonality links conservation on all continents. As habitat—the currency of wildlife—erodes and fragments, populations become increasingly isolated. Some parcels merely offer transient asylum, while others may receive formal protection as refuges and parks. Ironically, these safe havens may become victims of their protected wildlife, especially overabundant large herbivores. Balance and human benevolence remain necessary for all of earth's life to persevere.

A century ago when the National Elk Refuge was established, things were far different. Large mammal species were imperiled across the United States due to the crush of Euro-American exploitation in a land where former bounty had seemed endless. Bison and elk were seen as competitors with cattle and sheep, and predators were viewed as a scourge on the land. Passenger pigeons and egrets were shot without restriction for food and plumes. As the emerging art and science of wildlife management evolved from production of favored species (those popular with sportsmen or as food) to a more enlightened understanding of the interrelationships of all species in ecosystems, state and federal laws and conservation programs encompassed nongame species like songbirds, amphibians, and carnivores.

The National Wildlife Refuge System Improvement Act was long-overdue legislation that incorporated these ecological precepts into conservation policy. No longer can management of national wildlife refuges remain so narrowly focused as to produce an abundance of a few species at the expense of the diversity and health of other life-forms.

The 2012 federal court ruling instructed the U.S. Fish and Wildlife Service that the National Elk Refuge must embark in a new direction consistent with Congress's intent. As the refuge's wildlife biologist for twenty-two years, I saw firsthand the trade-offs of farming elk to the detriment of their habitat and health. Although I find it preferable for policy reform to come from within, after years of resistance and delay, it was rewarding to see a high court's decision affirm that the refuge's management practices must comply with the law as well as with the scientific evidence for improved stewardship of the public's natural resources.

Unfortunately, the appellate court did not mandate a timetable, and the refuge has yet to begin phasing out winter feeding. More elk were fed in the years 2014 and 2015 than in any year since 1998. Refuge woodlands and shrublands remain under siege. Just as many citizens want to see measurable progress, I trust that the patience of federal judges is limited too.

SIXTEEN

FOUR DECADES LATER

> I just wish the world was twice as big
> and half of it was still unexplored.
> —David Attenborough, *Life on Earth*

If asked, most people will name their favorite animal. Mine is perhaps the most extraordinary mountaineer to ever live—the mountain goat. I've admired the shaggy beast and its lofty life-style for many years. But one singular August morning captured the wonder of the animal's realm. Beyond the ragged divide I straddled between two glacier-gouged canyons in Montana's Bitterroot Mountains, a broad cirque basin sprawled in the yawning shadow of two majestic peaks. Through binoculars and tripod-mounted spotting scope, I scanned sweeps of granite, flowered gardens, and melting snowdrifts for the Old Man of the Mountains. Rewarding my squinting, a display of wildlife burst from that grand mosaic.

"Eeeeek," a pika announced her presence from a sunny balcony, then returned to stockpiling hay for the upcoming winter. Gray-crowned rosy finches flicked in and out of cracks in cliffs where they may have raised another year's brood of chicks. A half mile distant, a dark object caught my eye. Popping like a periscope from a jumble of boulders, a wolverine came bounding my way. Like a game of hide-and-seek, he would navigate hidden pathways and reappear ever closer to appraise his intended prey. One of the hoary marmots spotted the would-be assassin. He whistled a high-pitched alarm to his less vigilant companions, who were cavorting on snowbanks or grazing glacier lilies. When the hunter materialized within striking range, the ten-pound rodents vanished as if swallowed by the mountain. After a brief investigation, the wolverine scaled an escarpment as steep as a cow's face. Faster than seemed possible, he was out of sight. The only thing missing was a *Nature* film crew.

As this drama unfolded, a swarm of ladybugs swirled around me. Some crawled on my legs and arms. One nipped my neck as if mistaking the green-parka-clad intruder for an oversized aphid. Surveying all of this from a wedge of granite encircled by pink-petaled heather and yellow-plumed groundsels was a lone billy goat. Like a benign ruler of a magic kingdom, maybe he, like me, regarded everything in perfect order on his mountain.

♠

That was in 1974, a year that I spent every week backpacking through 150 square miles of the Bitterroot Mountains, from late May—when the first goat kids are born—until snow drove me out in late October. I'd leaped at the chance to spend much of three years at altitude studying the animal's ecology for a graduate degree at the University of Montana. Those five- or six-day, off-trail trips in 1974 traversed the ridges dividing the range's parallel canyons. None was more memorable than this August trek through some of the most goat-worthy country the Selway-Bitterroot Wilderness Area offers.

Four decades later, I returned during the last week of July to this place that lodged in my heart and launched my science career. Would it rekindle cherished memories? But foremost, would I find descendants of my old friends still gracing the heights?

To be exact, 2013 was thirty-nine years later. But once you qualify for the Medicare rolls, a year here or there can get lost, like gold dust sifting through a saloon floor's cracks. Were it not for her asthma, my wife, Diana, would have joined me. By default, this trip was like the one in 1974. I was on my own—with one exception. She insisted I pack a cell phone.

I'm not a fan of cell phones. Secure in the mountaineering skills and bushcraft I'd nurtured over the years, I never saw the need to own one. Such techie devices seem like a pointless crutch. Besides, I enjoy the uninterrupted sounds of wind through trees, tumbling water, and the wild critters' calls. A sure sign you're alone in the wilderness is that you don't hear human voices. If you do, you're either talking to yourself or to the rocks. Unless, of course, a pesky cell phone rings.

The trek began early on July 24 at the St. Mary's Peak trailhead (elevation 6,800 feet). Three and a half miles in, I left the trail and busted through a tangle of dwarf whitebark pine and subalpine fir to the shoulder of St. Mary at 9,000 feet. Nearly three miles west towered the Heavenly Twins, aptly named granite spires that are among the highest summits in the northern Bitterroot Range. In between sprawled two glacial cirques. The nearest one sheltered St. Mary's Lake, my intended campsite. The route there plunged 1,200 feet through scattered forest, downfall, loose rock, and beargrass to the basin, followed by scrambling across outcrops, ledges, and ravines to the lake.

Such treacherous travel with a full pack is a writer's bonanza, as colorful adjectives randomly bubble forth. But the three words that kept coming to mind were *big*, *brutal*, and *dry*. The country—and how much remained to be traveled—seemed bigger than I remembered. Things often seem bigger when we're children than when we're adults. Although I was an adult in 1974, the land now seemed more expansive than before, perhaps because I was driven during that earlier time when my boots ate up the mountains in big chunks. I was on a mission then to learn all I could about mountain goats and the wonderland they called home. It was all so new and exciting and challenging . . . in a heady way.

♠

During the steep descent to the lake, I quickly got a wake-up call. A loose rock rolled beneath a carelessly placed step, resulting in a tumble. *Pay attention!* I redoubled my concentration to plan each step.

Not once in the journals I kept from 1974 do I mention the mountaineering being difficult, surely not brutal. Not the climbing with sixty pounds strapped on my back, nor navigating boulder fields and cliff ledges under the constant resistance of gravity, day after twelve-hour day. My notes only recount the animals I saw, with lengthy narratives detailing their behavior: what plants they nibbled, where they traveled and bedded, and the peaceful interactions punctuated by aggression I observed among group members.

I had planned to train for this journey, knowing that it would be grueling and my staying power would be tested. But almost three weeks before my departure, I landed a wicked head cold and sinus infection—something for which my doctor prescribed antibiotics and Diana prescribed forgoing my morning runs until I recovered. Starting a couple of weeks before the trip, I had intended to load a sixty-pound sandbag into my backpack and hike up and down a mountain trail not far from our home a few times. Doesn't that sound like fun?

The week before leaving, I loaded the sandbag. With raised eyebrows and a fanny pack, Diana joined me on two of these training jaunts. On that first slog up the mountain, my hip joints screamed in protest, unaccustomed to bearing such weight. The second was better. Thanks to those training miles the week before, my hips merely ached when I reached St. Mary's Lake.

Dry was the third adjective that came to mind. The lack of recent precipitation had left the soil parched and dusty. In the Rockies, dry and hot seem to go together. Even at eight thousand to nine thousand feet, the temperature reached the eighties. Vegetation was senescing and remnant snow seemed scarcer than I remembered. Most of the beargrass had gone to seed; and although swathes of the signature plant of the Bitterroot high country, mountain heath, bore their bell-shaped, pink blooms, I found patches that were brown and brittle, maybe dead.

As I crested a final fold in the bedrock encircling St. Mary's Lake, I was stunned to see a fire ring in the shoreline meadow. An old ring, from years prior, but a fire ring nonetheless. Throughout 1974, I don't recall seeing any evidence of human presence during my off-trail mountaineering.

The next day, I struck out west, carrying just a daypack with spotting scope, tripod, camera, water, and food. I aimed to see as much of this country as daylight and my legs allowed, with designs on scaling the Heavenly Twins. In 1974 when I reached the south summit—the higher of the two at 9,282 feet—I was greeted by wraparound views of peaks and lakes and by a swarm of ladybug beetles that alighted on me. This time, a flurry of delicate white butterflies swirled like a tiny snowstorm at the top. Joining in were assorted bees and flies and a flight of winged ants.

From the roof of the world, I scanned four cirques whose glaciers had once ground headwalls that now shape these twin pinnacles. Glades of lilies, whistles of marmots, and the dog-toy squeaks of pikas treated my eyes and ears. I wasn't surprised to find no wolverines. They're elusive vagabonds rarely seen by the most seasoned mountaineers. But disturbingly, I couldn't spot a single mountain goat anywhere.

Even an old goat spotter, I suppose, can overlook an animal in this jumbled mosaic of wind-racked trees, splotches of meadow, and silvery granite and gneiss. But the clincher was that in three days I found no tracks or droppings, no beds or dust wallows. On a recent foray into Glacier National Park to photograph goats, tufts of their hair festooned wildflower stalks in a meadow traveled by the animals, as though the wild geraniums and coneflowers had been supplanted by a field of cotton. But here, not a wisp of shed hair fluttered from bushes or branches marking the white climbers' passage. These observations only reinforced my mostly fruitless forays in search of the Bitterroots' cliff dwellers in recent winters. Although the land itself was much as I remembered, the wilderness seemed empty without its goats.

In 1974 I recorded fifteen observations of the animals totaling thirty-eight individuals in the same area I would scour in 2013. Ogling every fold and undulation, every ledge and meadow, I found that the trails goats have traveled for millennia remained, just not the descendants of those who made them. In the past, I need only look longer or more intently, and these mountain monarchs would appear. Now I was saddened to find otherwise.

The Bitterroots do not stand alone. Over the past half century, numbers have dwindled across Montana's historic goat ranges. What survey data exists suggests that populations have plummeted by 85 percent in the Bob Marshal Wilderness. Shocking declines have likewise occurred in the Swan Range and Pintler Ranges and in the Great Bear and Scapegoat Wildernesses—all former strongholds of the Old Man of the Mountains.

We know that herds that for generations have been anchored on the same pile of rocks typically have low birthrates and survival of young—a consequence of lives spent living on the edge. Studies from Montana to Washington, Alberta, and British Columbia conclude that excessive hunting in the past and our commercial intrusions for energy, timber, and even recreation sometimes were incompatible with the goats' persistence and reclusive lifestyle.

Why do depleted herds often fail to recover after wildlife managers have reined in hunting quotas? Does the animal's placid outward appearance mask physiological stress inflamed by snowmobiles and helicopters invading their world? Are predators the culprits, as often implicated in declines of other herbivore species we hold dear? How then is it that before the recent arrival of Euro-Americans, the West's large carnivores and their prey both flourished in far greater abundance than now? And is the changing climate—warming twice as fast at the highest altitudes and latitudes than here below—a challenge for this cold-adapted, Ice Age survivor? Questions are many, but answers are few about the animal's prospects. We have much to learn to conserve this icon of the alpine that has lived and died out of sight and out of mind from most of us.

On my return from the Bitterroots, I related these things to Diana. She took it all in, hearing the anxiety in my voice. After a moment, she asked if I would go back to St. Mary's, the Heavenly Twins, and their goat range again. I considered the question and replied, "I'll return to that place when the mountain goats do."

AFTERWORD

IN THE WILD

There are days in the high country—ebullient days—when sunlight reflects so brightly off snow and ice and crystalline stone that it can burn your eyes. The pinks, lemons, lavenders, and whites of the wildflowers dazzle. Water that dances and tumbles down glistening granite swells mirrors the scenery in still pools and tranquil ponds.

When day lengths shorten, autumn alpenglow filters through the golden needles of alpine larch as richly as refracted light through a precious stone. The needles change from their summer dress of lime green so quickly that I wonder if I missed a day or two. But I was there the whole time, tromping through the high country in search of mountain goats or sheep or elk, or just drinking in the freshest air to be found.

There are evenings spent sipping cocoa on a cushion of sedges in front of my tent and evenings I wish the last light would linger on and on. I watch the shadows of the larch and whitebark pines march across glades of mountain heath and heather, transforming their bell-shaped flowers from rosy pink to crimson then burgundy. In the glow of dusk, the shrill whistles of hoary marmots—sentinels of the cirques—and tweeterings of rosy finches sound taps. Pitched at the margin of a glacier-carved basin, spires and arêtes dwarf my tiny cerulean shelter. Their shadows smother the failing sunlight from the alpine dusk, only to be replaced by the radiance of a star-studded night. When daybreak shimmers across a glaze of frost, the sun's radiant warmth repaints the land.

I am simply awed at times by the immensity and grandeur of it all. Perhaps protohumans, thousands and millions of years ago, felt the same: like merely fragile specks on the land. That is what wild places and the wild things that live there do for us; they return us to our roots and a more harmonious place on the earth.

Acknowledgments

Storytelling is an ancient and defining trait of our species. Our stories define the arc of our lives and, in sum, make each life unique, like no other. Mine are the product of times with special people, places, and life-forms that were too memorable to remain in my head and seldom shared with others along the way. I chose to put them on paper to entertain others and perhaps to inspire greater affection and connection to wild things and the places they live, knowing there is no better way to appreciate and engage with nature than being "out there."

Although most are original stories, five of the chapters are adaptations of previously printed works. "Snowbound" and part of "Old Garbage Gut" first appeared in *Wildlife on the Wind: A Field Biologist's Journey and an Indian Reservation's Renewal* (Logan: Utah State University Press, 2010). A portion of "The Circle" first appeared in *Where Elk Roam: Conservation and Biopolitics of Our National Elk Herd* (Guilford CT: Lyons Press, 2011). A condensed version of "Empty Forests" and "Four Decades Later" were published in *Big Sky Journal*, in the winter 2011 and the summer 2014 issues, respectively.

To bring this collection to its final form, I thank Don Burgess for his review of the manuscript. His insights were valuable as always. My wife and chief proponent, Diana, likewise read each draft chapter. With the eye of a voracious reader, her suggestions also brought clarity to the writing.

Finally, such collections of stories are not at the top of publishers' want lists. I thank the University of Nebraska Press and my editor, Rob Taylor, for taking on this project and shepherding it through the publication process.

IN THE OUTDOOR LIVES SERIES

Pacific Lady: The First Woman to Sail
Solo across the World's Largest Ocean
by Sharon Sites Adams with Karen J. Coates

Kayaking Alone: Nine Hundred Miles from
Idaho's Mountains to the Pacific Ocean
by Mike Barenti

Bicycling beyond the Divide:
Two Journeys into the West
by Daryl Farmer

Beneath Blossom Rain: Discovering
Bhutan on the Toughest Trek in the World
by Kevin Grange

The Hard Way Home: Alaska Stories of
Adventure, Friendship, and the Hunt
by Steve Kahn

Almost Somewhere: Twenty-Eight
Days on the John Muir Trail
by Suzanne Roberts

Stories from Afield: Adventures
with Wild Things in Wild Places
by Bruce L. Smith

To order or obtain more information on these
or other University of Nebraska Press titles,
visit nebraskapress.unl.edu.

CPSIA information can be obtained at www.ICGtesting.com
Printed in the USA
LVOW08s1313130816

500251LV00007B/225/P